COTTAGE MAYHEM

Phantom Publishing 2011

First Edition

Cottage Mayhem

Phantom Publishing 2011

First Edition

ISBN: 978-1-257-95901-3

This book is dedicated to my beloved son Paul.
Daddy loves you always and forever.

Table of Contents:

Introduction.

Welcome to the wonderful and excitingly fun world of backyard and cottage mayhem. Upon starting this book, I found many resources to be aspiring but so very few put many of these fun and entertaining ideas into a single resource. So I decided to compile some of the ones I found to be most fun and entertaining and place them together in a single book. We will cover the famous classics, all the way up to some of the newer ones, and play with some experimental concepts as well.

Like many outdoor activities and hobbies there is always safety risks and concerns which must be followed to ensure everyone remains safe and has the most enjoyable time while doing these experiments. Therefore is it vital to ensure that all these activities are done under the supervision of an adult and that all necessary safety precautions are followed. In the next section we will discuss the various common safety precautions a little more in detail.

A note to parents. Although many of these activities are designed and prepared with the expectation that younger children may be participating in them, it is assumed that an adult will be supervising children through all the steps in the process. Some steps and processes it is simply unsafe for children to be doing themselves or unattended. It is your responsibility to ensure the safety of your child and others around while performing these projects and experiments.

Safety Precautions

For many of the described experiments there will be use of some form of propellant, ignition source, or other chemical reactive substance and/or situation in order for the project to be a success. This being said, it is necessary for some common precautions to be taken through the duration of these experiments.

While handling any and all chemicals it is vital to ensure you are always wearing hand, eye, skin, and face protection. This means using protective goggles/face shielding. Surgical/rubber gloves, an over coat/lab jacket. Handling chemical mixtures can be extremely volatile even in the safest of situations. It is always better to be safe than sorry when it comes to handling chemical substances and propellants.

Never substitute. The given directions call for certain components for a reason, it is never safe or advisable to substitute items, chemicals, fuels, or building materials with other items. Be it or lesser, equal, or better grade.

Remove unused fuels/chemicals from test and firing areas. If your project calls for lighter fluid as the propellant, add the required fuel and remove the extra fuel from the area, it is generally advisable to keep unused fuels / chemicals at least 50 feet from firing area.

Follow the directions! For many reading this book, you will already be familiar with a lot of these concepts. Perhaps you have made some of these projects already. There is never an excuse for taking short cuts and not following the directions thoroughly. You have the information at your fingertips, so there is no reason any of these steps should be skipped. I am a person who dislikes unnecessary work, so please rest assured if a step is written in the directions, it is there for a reason, please make sure it is included. *Failure to follow the directions as specified may result in the project failing to function properly, or in more serious cases can cause harm or even death to the participants.*

A word on structural projects. In some projects described here it will detail and include structural plans, if you have no previous experience in construction or building items of stability, some of these projects may be unsafe to attempt. When fastening items to supports, always make sure they are correctly and securely connected to avoid what could become a fatal flaw in design.

Keep participants out of the firing area, For items such as cannons, mortars or other items where propellant and fuels are used in the project, keep all observers or patrons not required to be involved in the project/experiment at a safe distance away from the firing/test area. Never allow young children to handle or light propellants/fuel mixtures.

Use common sense. I know this may sound ridiculous to even have to be mentioned, but with no surprise if it is not mentioned, someone, somewhere will attempt something stupid and end up injuring themselves. With all projects and activities like this, it requires a little bit of common sense. For example, when building a Zip line, or Rope bridge, just because you can run the zip line across a 200 foot drop chasm, that does not make it a good idea, ***and should not be attempted.*** With projects that include propellants, gun powder, or other combustible items, it is ***NEVER*** advisable or remotely recommended to "Increase the amount of fuel" into any mixture. So this being said do not double up on recommended amounts of propellant or fuel. This can be extremely dangerous and even explosively lethal if enough fuel is added to any mixture.

When in doubt, don't do it. This falls into the common sense aspect. However it is worth taking the time to mention it clearly. If you are unsure of any aspect of a project do not attempt to do it. Your personal safety and those around you is never worth the risk in an attempt to have a bit of fun. If you are unsure of something within a project ensure you seek the necessary advice or assistance to ensure it is safely completed.

Safety Recap:

- Always use protective equipment, especially when dealing with fuels or chemical mixtures.
- Never substitute items, materials, fuels, or chemicals.
- Remove unused fuels/chemicals from firing area.
- Follow the directions thoroughly. Do not skip steps.
- Ensure all structural projects are safely and securely built. Ensure they are properly fastened and secured.
- Keep observers at a safe distance from firing area, never allow children to handle or light fuel/propellant mixtures.
- Use common sense. If your "gut instinct" is telling you it's a bad idea, it probably is.
- Don't add more fuel to any mixtures other than the recommended amounts.
- Always use fall protection when working from heights
- Never attempt a project or step unless you are confident you can accomplish it without risk to yourself or others.
- When building structures which are covered ensure you have proper support for the weight being placed above you, improper support can and will result in cave ins.

Section 1

Cannons, Mortars, Rockets and Ballistics

In this section we will be covering all projects relating to Cannons, mortars, rockets and other various ballistic elements. The common goal is to produce a final product which will project items at high velocity great distances.

Important Safety Information for This Section

This section deals with 2 very important safety concerns, first is the extremely high velocities of which objects will be shot at. Ensuring the targeted areas are clear of people, animals and buildings if extremely important. Second is the nature of the designs and builds which are detailed through this chapter. These designs have been tried and tested as exactly detailed. It is crucial people who attempt to build these projects never deviate or modify the designs, doing so could result in fatal injuries. It is vital that safety equipment and protective gear always be use when constructing and using any built projects. Failing to do so could result in injury or death. Children must always be supervised when involved in these projects, and must never attempt or be allowed to use or build any described projects without adult supervision.

For cannon, mortar or other tube design projects it is very important to never look down the barrel of a loaded or charged project. On this note, it is also extremely important to never reach down or in to a charged or loaded project for any reason. If maintenance must be done on the project, you must always unload and discharge the project before any work may be done, this means releasing the propellant and removing the projectile before you start repairs or maintenance.

For all ballistic projectile projects, always ensure the area where the project being aimed and fired is clear of people, animals and buildings. The projectiles in these projects will be traveling at extremely high velocities and will cause serious injury or death if they come into contact with living beings.

Potato Cannon

The Potato Cannon is a classic and a favorite for cottage goers. With its simplicity to build and easy to get materials it is a North American tradition for cottagers all around.

Materials Required:

1x	2 inch diameter schedule 40 PVC piping – 36 inch length
1x	3 inch diameter schedule 40 PVC piping – 15 inch length
1x	3 to 2 inch diameter reducing schedule 40 PVC piping bushing
1x	Can PVC primer
1x	Can PVC cement
1x	3 inch coupling one side threaded
1x	Roll Duct Tape
1x	3 inch diameter threaded schedule 40 PVC end cap
1x	Flint Lamp Starter (Available in hardware/camping stores)
1x	4 foot 1inch diameter wooden dowel/broom handle
1x	Electric Drill inc. 1/8 & 5/16 Drill bits
1x	Hack saw
1x	File
1x	Can of aerosol hair spray
1+x	Protective equipment including eye, ear and glove protection.
1x	Bag of Potatoes

Instructions:

1. Clear a working space sufficient for this project, a work bench or table of 4 foot by 3 foot should be the minimum space allotted.
2. Place all materials and equipment on the table and set materials out in the fashion detailed below. (Fig.1.a)

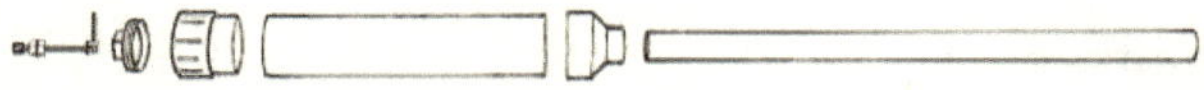

Fig.1.a

3. Use the hacksaw to cut all the PVC piping to the desired specified lengths.
4. Use the file to smooth and taper the newly sawn edges of the PVC piping. On the 2 inch PVC piping section you must file one end to a sharpened edge this will serve to cut the potatoes to shape when rammed into the cannons tubing.
5. Using the PVC primer prime all the respectable areas of the cannon. This is where the PVC will be joined using the PVC cement.
6. Allow PVC primer to dry thoroughly.
7. Using the PVC cement, join the 3 to 2 inch reducing pipe bushing to the 3 inch piping. When using the PVC cement ensure all areas to be cemented are cleaned and clear of debris. Follow instructions as listed on PVC cement, ensure a solid and good bond if made to all PVC joins.
8. Allow PVC cement to dry thoroughly overnight, ensure drying area is well ventilated.
9. Using the PVC cement, cement the 3 inch couplings unthreaded end (threaded on other side) to the 3 inch piping section. Again making sure the cementing area is clean and clear of debris. Further ensure no PVC cement comes into contact with the threading of the coupling. As you will be unable to close the end cap if this happens. Again allow to thoroughly dry overnight.
10. Using PVC cement yet again, cement the 2 inch wide, 36 inch long piping section to the 2 to 3 inch reducing piping cementing the end of the piping which is not sharpened (untapered). Again allowing for it to thoroughly dry overnight.

11. Taking the end threaded cap, drill a hole 1/8 or 5/16 inch in the center of the cap, this hole must match the diameter of the flint lamp starter. Ensure you do not cause any cracks or breaches in the end cap while drilling.
12. Taking apart the flint lamp starter, assemble the flint starter through the newly drilled hole in the end threaded cap. This will serve as your trigger/ignition method for the cannon, so be careful in assembly.
13. Allow entire project to dry completely before testing with live fuel. Failing to do so will result in a catastrophic failure of device, and can be potentially lethal.
14. For added safety use Duct tape to thickly layer the exterior piping of the cannon everywhere with the exception of the threaded end cap and sharpened tapered end of piping. This will prevent shrapnel in the case of a cannon failure.

Safety

- The potato cannon fires with a large amount of force, enough to cause serious or fatal injury, never point the device at people or animals.
- Always ensure the end cap is completely screwed on before firing
- Never over charge the cannon with propellant (in this case hair spray) only a small amount of hair spray is required for the cannon to operate at full efficiency, over filling will cause a mis fire and possible damage to the cannon.
- The cannon when fired produces recoil (kick back) always ensure it is held on to tightly or secured properly before firing.
- Always use proper protection when using this device, it can produce loud amounts of noise, so hearing, eye and hand protection is required at all times when using this device.
- Ensure the target area is well clear of obstructions. Always keep the target area clear and ensure you are aware of what is within the field of range for at least 300 yards ahead of target, and 25 yards behind. Remember if it is within the line of sight of the cannons firing end, it can be hit by the cannons projectiles.

Using / Firing

1. Remove threaded end cap
2. Using the dowel or broom handle push a potato down the barrel of the cannon, the sharpened edge at the end will cut away excess potato as it is pushed down the cannons barrel. Ensure the potato fits snug and tight around all edges of the piping, if there is gaps or openings the resulting explosive gas will blow past causing a launch failure, if the potato's do not fit correctly, you can alternatively use news paper to pack down at the end to create the desired effect before fitting with a potato.
3. Spray a short 1-2 second burst of hair spray into the firing chamber (3 inch PVC piping section)
4. Immediately put end cap onto firing chamber tightening it securely
5. Take aim with cannon, using care and caution never to point it at persons, animals or structures.
6. Twist the Flint starter to fire the cannon!

Final Thoughts

This is an all time classic worth hours of fun for the entire family. Ensure to check and clean the barrel and firing chamber after every few shots, as the hair spray fuel mixture has a tendency to cause build up and will cause the threaded end cap to stick after a few shots. Using the dowel/ram rod you can attach a rag with a bit of water and soap to clean out the barrel of the cannon. Ensure cannon barrel is dry before use again.

Tennis Ball Mortar

A simple and fun project for a boring summers afternoon. Cheap and easy to build, making it another favorite amongst backyarders and cottage goers alike.

Materials Required

3x Cardboard potato chip cans (such as processed potato chips)

1x File

1x Roll of Duct Tape

1x Tin snips or very sharp sturdy shop scissors

1x 3/16 inch diameter drill bit / hole punch

1x 4 inch diameter PVC piping, equal to length of 3 potato chip cans

1x Bottle of liquid lighter fluid, butane gas fuel does not work for this experiment.

1+x Tennis ball(s) (However many you intend on firing)

1x Long handled BBQ lighter / long handled matches

1x Protective gear, including eye, ear and hand protection.

7x Large stones / bricks to hold mortar in place.

Instructions

1. Taking the three potato chip tubes, set one aside to be the "Base" This specific tube will act as the firing chamber of the mortar.
2. Taking the remaining 2 potato chip tubes, using the tin snips or scissors cut out a 1 inch diameter hole in the center o the tin bases of the tubes. Ensure it is as immediate centered as possible. The cut out holes should be 50% of the whole tin base. These holes create baffles within the mortar tubing.
3. File the newly cut out holes edges smoothing them so they are safe to handle without being cut.
4. Assemble all tubing together with the baffled tubes at the top using duct tape (Fig.2.a), ensure you layer duct tape layers at least 5 times thick to ensure structural stability. Ensure all joints are secured and not leaking, if problems are encountered with leaks apply more duct tape around joins.

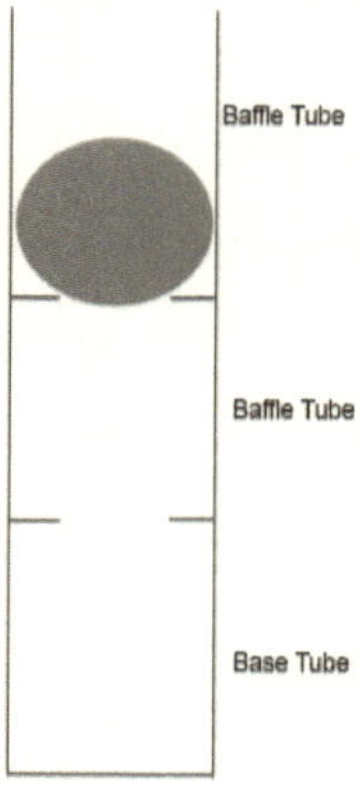

Fig.2.a

5. Using the 4 inch diameter PVC piping fit the newly taped mortar tubing into the PVC piping and ensure it fits snugly, if there is additional space between mortar tubing and PVC piping apply more duct tape to fill the gap.
6. Drill a hole 3/16 inch diameter 1 inch above the base end of the tubing. Ensuring this hole is drilled through both PVC piping and mortar tubes. Make sure it is clear of all obstructions as this will serve as your firing hole.

Using / Firing

1. Using the liquid lighter fluid, pour ½ teaspoon of fuel down the barrel of the mortar tubing, ensuring it does not hit the baffled edging within the tubing. This can be tricky and may take some time to perfect, never use more fuel than called for although it may not seem like enough adding more can be extremely dangerous.
2. Once fuel is at the base end of the mortar tubing, place the tennis ball in the mortar end, the ball will fall down tubing and come to a rest at the first baffled edge.
3. While holding the tennis ball in place, shake the mortar tubing thoroughly to spread the fuel through the mortar tubing, this allows for the fuel to be spent evenly.
4. Place mortar into firing position using heavy rocks or bricking to hold into place, leaving the firing hole open and clear of all obstructions. ***Important*** Never hold the mortar while firing, this can be extremely dangerous.
5. Using a long handled lighter or fireplace match light the firing hole, this will in turn cause the contained gas to ignite spending the fuel and force the tennis ball out of the mortar tubing.
6. Repeat steps 1-5 for further shots.

Final Thoughts

The tennis ball mortar is a simple easy and fun time killer for those summer days. However with all projects that call for fuel or chemical combustion care and caution is necessary when using such devices. Always remember to never add more fuel than what mixture calls for, and never hold mortar tubing while firing. Keep persons at a safe distance and wear proper eye ear and hand protection when using this device. Never aim within distance of persons animals of buildings. Never look down the barrel or muzzle of such devices as projectiles leave at extremely high velocities. If the mortar fails to ignite remove all ignition sources ie – wipe down inner mortar tube for fuel and restart from Step 1. Getting the hang of fueling tennis ball mortars can take some practice to get it right, for best results try to get some fuel by the ignition hole for best results and ensure firing hole is clear from obstruction.

Hydro Rocket

The Hydro Rocket is a backyard rocket enthusiasts dream. Cheap, quick and easy to setup, this fun little lesson in physics is sure to entertain young and old alike.

Materials Required

1x	#4 Rubber stopper, 1 inch in diameter and length
1x	Inflating needle (for inflating soccer balls, volley balls)
1x	Super glue
1x	Duct tape
1x	8-10 inches of 3/16 outer diameter copper tubing
1x	2 litre plastic pop bottle
4x	3x2 inch Balsa wood
1x	Wooden Block – 12 inches square
1x	Air pump – foot powered
1x	18 inches of 1 inch diameter dowel
1x	Paper towel roll
1x	Drill with 1/16 and 5/32 inch drill bits
1x	3 inch wood screw

Instructions

Stopper Assembly

1) Taking the #4 Rubber stopper, drill a 3/16 inch hole ½ way through the middle of the larger sided end of the stopper. Next drill a 5/32 inch hole ½ way through the other smaller end in the middle until the two drill holes meet. (Fig.3.a)
2) Straighten the copper tubing and insert it into the rubber stoppers 5/32 inch hole.
3) Insert the inflation needle into the other end of the rubber stoppers 1/16 inch hole so the needle passes into the copper tubing.

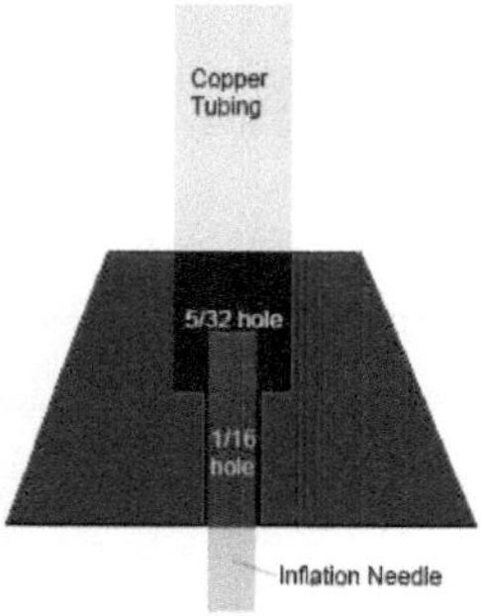

Rocket Assembly

1) Using the 4x Balsa Wood pieces make Fins for the rocket by evenly attaching them to the bottle using either super glue or duct tape (or both for best results)
2) Attach the paper towel roll to the rocket using duct tape so the roll runs up and down the bottle. (Fig.3.b)

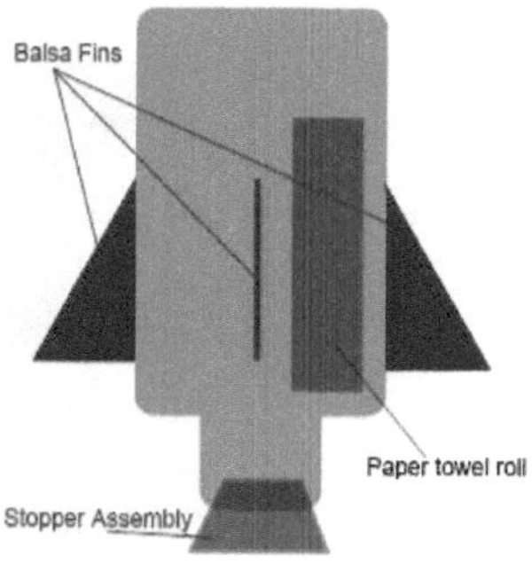

(Fig.3.b)

Launch Platform

1) Using the wooden block assemble Stopper assembly to the middle of the wooden block, by attaching the air pumps nozzle to the inflation needle contained within the stopper assembly. Glue the air pump/stopper assembly to the middle of the wooden platform using the Super glue so the copper tubing it pointing outwards from the wooden block platform.
2) Allow the Pump/stopper assembly to fully dry.
3) Attach the bottle rocket assembly to the platform and mark where the center of the paper towel roll matches up with the wooden block platform assembly. This is where you are going to fix the dowel to the platform, so make sure it is accurately measured.
4) Screw the dowels end to the marked spot on the wooden platform assembly using the wood screw. This dowel is to add stability to the rocket while on the platform. (Fig.3.c)

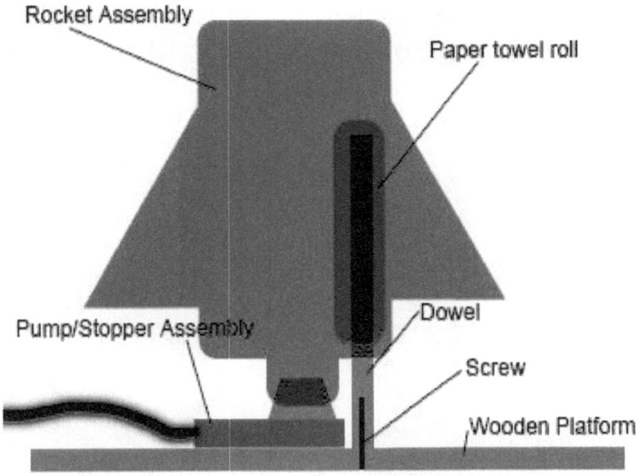

(Fig.3.c)

Launching

1) Connect air pump to assembly.
2) Fill bottle rocket ½ full with water, attach stopper assembly firmly to bottle rocket.
3) Invert the platform assembly with bottle rocket attached and place in launch area.

4) Using air pump steadily pump air into the bottle rocket, the amount of air required to build up enough pressure to launch the rocket varies depending on the seal between the stopper assembly and the bottle and the amount of water within the bottle.

5) After enough pumps the bottles pressure will build great enough launching the bottle into the air.

Final Thoughts

The Hydro rocket is fun for all ages and relatively safe compared to many projects in this book. It is highly recommended to try this project. But beware this activity is sure to get everyone wet. Use safety and common sense while operating devices like this. Ensure the rocket is never pointed towards people, animals or buildings. Always make sure there is a safe area for the bottle to land. Large fields are best for this activity as there is minimal chance of the bottle falling onto other people or property. Always make sure children are supervised while doing this activity. Proper protection is required for this activity.

The Super Sling

The super sling is one of the simplest and easy projects to make. With the simple application of elasticity you can launch medium sized objects to great distances with ease.

Materials Required

1x	50 feet of surgical tubing (stretchable rubber tubing)
1x	12x24 inch denim patch
1x	Spool of sewing thread
1x	Sewing needle
2x	Tree(s) or Posts 8-10 feet in distance of each other.

Instructions

1) Cut out ½ inch holes in each corner of the denim patch, 1 inch in from the corners of the denim patch. Reinforce holes by sewing the cut corners using sewing needle and thread. (Fig.4.a)
2) Cut Surgical tubing into 4x lengths of 12.5 inches each.
3) Securely tie each length of surgical tubing to a reinforced corner hole of the denim patch.
4) Tie 2x surgical tubing ends (on side where denim is 12 inches, not 24) to one Tree/Post, Tying higher on the tree or post will result in a greater angle thus allowing projectile to travel further. Recommended tubing is tied 3 foot distance from one another and bottom tie be 5 feet from the ground. – Ensure all ends are Secured properly.
5) Repeat step 4 to other side and tubing ends with second tree.

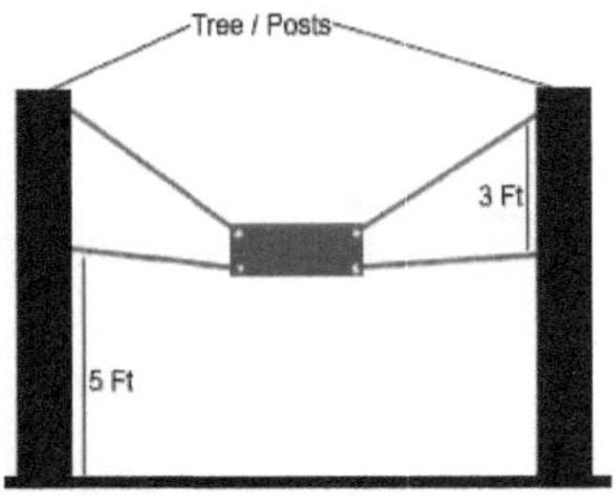

(Fig.4.a)

Using / Firing

1) Load a medium sized object such as a rock or other suitable projectile into the reinforced denim patch.
2) Pull denim patch back and down stretching the surgical rubber tubing in the process, while holding projectile in the denim patch. Important – Do not over stretch the rubber tubing, this can cause the tubing to snap and cause injury to operator or other observers.
3) Release the denim patch to have projectile fly into the direction the super sling is pointed.

Final Thoughts

The super sling is a very easy and entertaining device able to launch objects great distances by simple elasticity. However with all project and devices which send object air bound at high velocities care and caution must be used in the operation of the devices. Never aim or point the super sling at persons, animals or buildings, always ensure the target firing range is clear of obstructions and other items which can harmed or damaged. Never over stretch the tubing, know the tubing limits as over stretching can cause the tubing to snap and result in injury of the operator or observers. Finally always use eye protection when operating this device, although it is unlikely a projectile will be sent backwards it is always possible and with high velocity projectiles it is always recommended to be safe than sorry.

Ping Pong Ball Cannon

This is a simpler version of the potato cannon using the same basic principles to accomplish its goal. To launch a ping pong ball great distances at a high velocity. This project is great for those afternoons where traditional ping pong simply just doesn't cut it.

Materials Required

1x	Paper towel roll
1x	Duct tape
1x	Pair of Scissors
1x	Long necked BBQ lighter
1x	Can of aerosol hair spray
1x	Ping pong ball (or more)

Instructions

1) Using the duct tape seal one end of the paper towel cardboard tubing.
2) Poke a hole using the scissors in the duct taped end large enough for the long necked BBQ lighter to fit into creating a good seal.
3) Insert the long necked lighter into the newly created hole in the duct tape end ensuring it creates a good seal. (Fig.5.a)
4) Spray the hair spray into the open end for 1-2 seconds, being careful not to soak the paper towel tubing.
5) Quickly drop the ping pong ball into the tubing also ensuring it create a fairly good seal (ensure it is not too tight)
6) Point the ping pong ball cannon in a safe direction and ignite the lighter, propelling the ping pong ball out of the cannon.

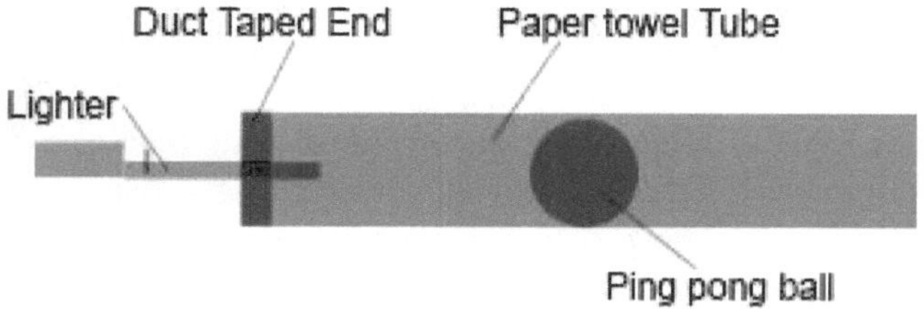

Fig.5.a

Final Thoughts

Always use care and caution when using propellant fuels. Hand and eye protection is required when using this device. When cardboard tubing becomes saturated with hair spray, leave to dry or discard and create a new one.

Section 2
Fireworks and Pyrotechnics

In this section we will be dealing with something all guys love, explosions. Through the following section we will detail the how and why things explode. From making your own black and flash powders to making M80's, bottle rockets and other fun pyrotechnics.

Important Safety Information for This Section

The Author takes no responsibility for person(s) who attempts any of these projects described within this section. This information is provided as an informational resource only, and **it is not advised to attempt any projects within this section.**

When dealing with explosive, reactive and hazardous chemicals and mixtures safety is first and foremost priority. Always use protective equipment, including but not limited to eye, ear, hand and body protection. When using chemicals or substances the area must always be well ventilated. Never smoke around, or keep flammable or explosive items in your work area. Never use metal tools to grind, mix or interact with compounds. Avoid sparks of any kind around compounds. Children are to never attempt any of the detailed projects or mixtures. Caution and care is to always be utilized if a person attempts these projects. Prior chemistry experience is required to understand how and why chemicals react the way they do. If you are uncertain or uncomfortable with the process never attempt to do it. And finally, when handling explosives, accidents can happen even in the safest of circumstances. Always be prepared for the worst case scenario with explosives, have a fire extinguisher on hand at all times, and be prepared to call the fire department if necessary.

Basics of Pyrotechnic Chemical Compounds

Pyrotechnics in general use two type of chemical compounds to produce there explosive effects, first is Gun powder or traditionally known as Black powder, the second is Flash powder. Both of these compounds are extremely volatile and extra attention and care is required when handling and using. When mixing chemicals and compounds it is important to never use metal, always use wooden items to mix compounds as this will avoid spark ignitions. Always use appropriate protective equipment at all times when handling explosive compounds.

Gunpowder vs. Flash powder

Although both compositions work very well, Flash powder is a newer composition specially designed with pyrotechnic applications in mind. This being said it is in general always recommended to buy/use Flash powder based fireworks. Gun powder although still highly explosive, burns slower and produces more smoke than actual bang.

Gunpowder

Gunpowder is one of the oldest and commonly used explosive compounds on earth, when fireworks were invented by the Chinese ages ago this chemical compound is what was used. In this project we will detail how to make gunpowder for pyrotechnic use.

Materials Required

	Sulfur
	Charcoal
	Potassium Nitrate (Saltpeter)
1x	Ball Mill
1x	Digital Scale

Instructions

The chemical breakdown (percentage by weight) for Gunpowder is:

75%	Potassium Nitrate
15%	Charcoal
10%	Sulfur

1. Using digital scale, weight out and measure all chemical components ensuring to keep separate, cleaning scale after each chemical is weighed.
2. Add Charcoal and Sulfur to ball mill, mill components for 4-6 hours.
3. Add Potassium Nitrate to charcoal and sulfur mixture in mill, mill for 24-48 hours. (Recommended 48 hours, the longer mixture is milled, the finer final product will be)
4. Remove resulting product from mill and store in a safe plastic container. Never store in metal or glass containers.

Flash Powder

Flash powder is a relatively new compound when compared to gunpowder, it is however designed with pyrotechnics in mind. The primary differences are that it is finer than traditional black/gunpowder, and flash powder uses a metal chemical element (usually aluminum powder) in its mixture for fuel, thus it burns faster. Flash powder also tends to create a louder bang than gunpowder. These two factors considered it is no surprise why flash powder is the choice for pyrotechnic enthusiasts. Flash powder, however, is more unstable and ignites easier than gunpowder so additional care and caution must always be used when handling flash powder compositions. Never make more flash powder than necessary, and never store flash powder.

Note: Only professional pyrotechnic manufactures should ever attempt to make or store flash powder compounds.

Materials Required

	Potassium Perchlorate
	Aluminum powder
1x	Paper
1x	Anti-static spray
1x	Ziploc bag
1x	Digital scale

Instructions

The chemical breakdown (percentage by weight) for flash powder is:

70%	Potassium Perchlorate
30%	Aluminum Powder

1. Prepare the work area and treat it with anti-static spray, use anti-static spray to treat Zip lock bag as well. Flash powder can be ignited by even the smallest static electrical spark, ensure you are thorough.

2. Weight out chemical components, cleaning scale for each chemical weighed.
3. Using piece of paper lay paper flat in work surface and place Potassium perchlorate on paper. Carefully placing Aluminum Powder on paper as well.
4. To mix compounds together slowly and evenly lift edges of paper one at a time, allowing the two chemicals to roll over top of one another, be sure to be thorough in mixing and that both compounds mix together evenly. Never use any other method or tools to mix flash powder. Mixing by hand using the paper method is safest.
5. Use anti static treated zip lock bag to store <u>temporarily</u> until ready to be used.

Firework fuses

What good is a firework without a safe way to light it? In this project we will detail how fuses for fireworks are made using a few simple and cheap items. Please note however when possible always try to buy commercial fuses as they are much more reliable.

Materials Required

	Gunpowder
	Water
1x	Ball of yarn
1x	Roll of paper towel
2x	Non metallic bowls

Instructions

1. Cut yarn to desired length of fuse(s)
2. Pour water into a bowl, pour a generous amount of gunpowder in a second bowl.
3. Take the cut yarn strands and soak in water bowl, ensuring entire strand is saturated with water, remove from water and allow excess water to drip away.
4. Take wet strands of yarn and place in gunpowder bowl ensuring gunpowder is thoroughly applied to wet strands of yarn.
5. Lay out paper towel and lay wet strands of gunpowder yarn mix in straight lengths on paper towel and allow to dry completely (over night is ideal)

Final Thoughts

As this is a "home brew" method before using fuses in fireworks of other pyrotechnic applications, be sure to burn some test fuses to determine how fast they burn. Always give yourself more time than estimated to retreat to a safe distance. When fuses are needed for projects it is always advisable to use commercial brand fuse instead of home made as they are much more reliable. If you wish to use an electrical ignition system model rocket engine starters work well to ignite fuses.

Bottle Rocket Fireworks

An all time classic firework. The bottle rocket is quick and easy to make, and entertaining for all. This project will explain how to build your own using almost all common household items.

Materials Required

(single bottle rocket)

1x	Wood skewer
1x	2.5 inch of commercial fuse
6x	1 inch of commercial fuse
1x	Page of news paper
1x	Super glue
1x	Glue stick
1x	Gunpowder or Flash powder
1x	Scissors

Instructions

1. Cut a piece of news paper into a 1 x 2 inch square. Also cut a 1.5 inch strip of news paper totaling the entire height of the news paper.
2. Using the glue stick glue one side of the news paper square. Take both lengths of fuses and wrap the 1 inch fuses so they surround the 2.5 inch fuse using the square of glued news paper square wrap the fuses together as tightly as possible without ripping the paper and allow to dry thoroughly. (Fig.6.a)

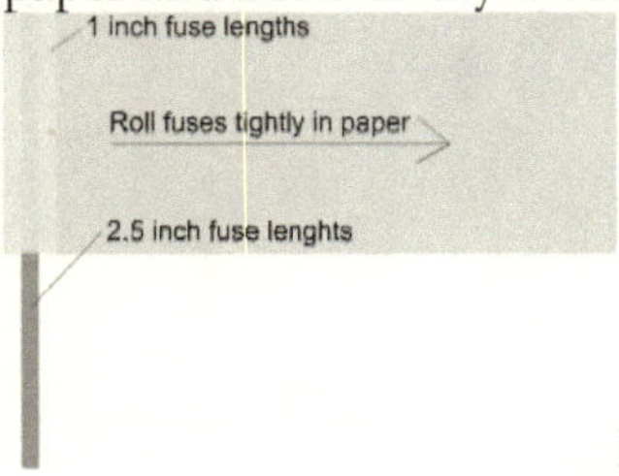

Fig.6.a

3. After fuse tube has dried take the 1.5 inch news paper strip, glue one inch of the strip using the glue stick, tightly wrap the fuse tube in it leaving the extra ½ inch of unglued space at the top of the fuse tube open. Allow to dry thoroughly. (Fig.6.b)

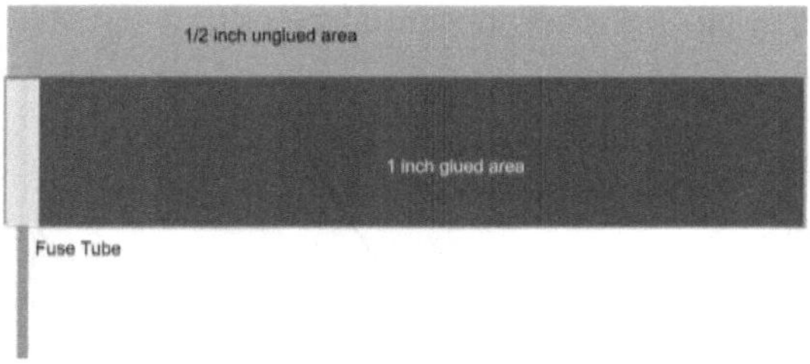

Fig.6.b

4. Once rocket tubing has finished drying, carefully pack the open top end with gunpowder or flash powder after powder is packed use a drop of superglue to seal powder in.
5. Using super glue put a couple drops on the side of the rocket tubing and glue to end of wood skewer and allow to dry.

Final Thoughts

Bottle rockets are fun and easy to make, always ensure proper safety equipment is used in the creation and use of these fun rockets, and never point at people, animals of buildings. Always use proper safety equipment when using or making anything pyrotechnic and always keep a safe distance when lighting pyrotechnic compounds.

American Cannon Cracker

The American cannon cracker quickly became popular just after the American civil war. Generally more powerful than the Chinese fire cracker this little puppy packs a lot of punch. Like all pyrotechnics safety and care must always be demonstrated when handling or using explosives, always use proper safety equipment at all time when in contact with pyrotechnics.

Materials Required

	Gunpowder
1x	4 inch fuse
1x	Scissors
1x	Glue stick
1+x	Letter/Legal paper
1x	Hard epoxy or lots of super glue

Instructions

1. Using the paper, glue stick and scissors, cut paper strips 3.5 inch in length. Using the Glue stick, glue a tube out of paper that is ½ inch inner diameter and 1/8 inch tube walls and allow to fully dry.
2. Once Paper tube(s) are dry, stand upright on a piece of paper and fill the bottom of the tube ¼ inch in thickness using the epoxy or superglue, be careful to not get the epoxy or super glue on the inside walls of the tube, and again allow to fully dry.
3. Once epoxy/superglue has completely dried and cured take Gunpowder composition and slowly pack in to tube using a non metallic packer, wooden towels work very well. Pack gunpowder composition into tube leaving ¼ inch at the top of the tube. Be careful not to over pack tubes!

4. Ensure fuse is in tubing and within gunpowder mixture slightly, using epoxy\super glue fill the remaining ¼ inch of tube, set to dry allowing to cure completely. (Fig.7.a)

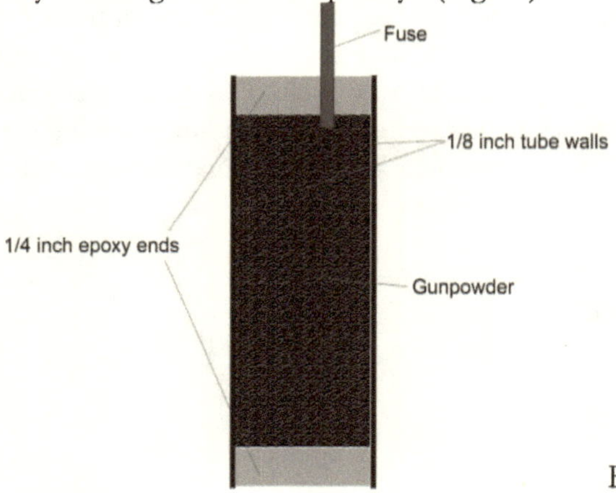

Fig.7.a

Final Thoughts

The American cannon cracker is a fantastic way to have some fun and make some noise. Remember to always follow the directions and not change or modify them, these are explosive compounds and are in all essence a small bomb, never increase these in size, doing so can be extremely dangerous and can cause serious injury or death, always use proper proactive equipment when handling or using pyrotechnics. Children should never be allowed to handle, manufacture, or use explosive compounds or pyrotechnics.

The Flash Cracker

This is one of the earliest fireworks that makes use of flash powder. With a very simple design but powerful display this has become a favorite for pyrotechnic makers for years, although many newer fireworks and designs have over taken this one in popularity, you can't beat the simplicity of this design. Like always, use of proper protective equipment is mandatory and Children should never be allowed to handle use or make any pyrotechnic projects or chemical compositions.

Materials Required

1x	4-6 inch of fuse
1x	Tissue paper
1x	Sheet regular paper
1x	String
1x	Glue stick
	Flash powder
	Scissors

Instructions

1. Using Tissue paper, place a small amount of flash powder on tissue paper and wrap fuse into flash powder using the tissue paper, being careful not to pack the flash powder but to ensure the powder is fairly tight (not too loose) use the string to tie the

wrapped flash powder and fuse together. (Fig.8.a)

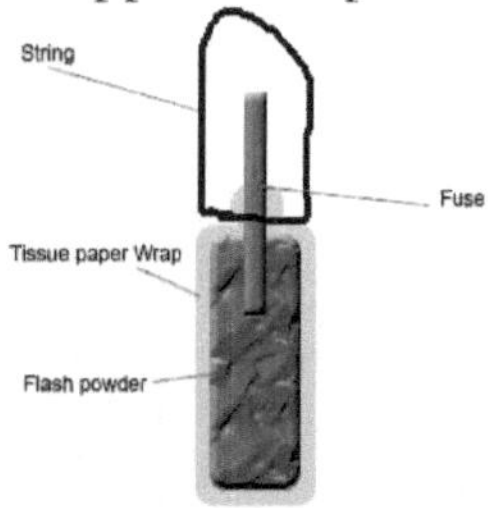

2. Using the glue stick and regular sheet of paper, glue a fair sized line, down the middle of the paper, after glue has been applied, place the Fuse/flash powder wrap at one end of the glued area and wrap the flash wrap in the piece of paper, creating a tube with the paper and Folding the bottom portion of extra paper. (Fig.8.b)

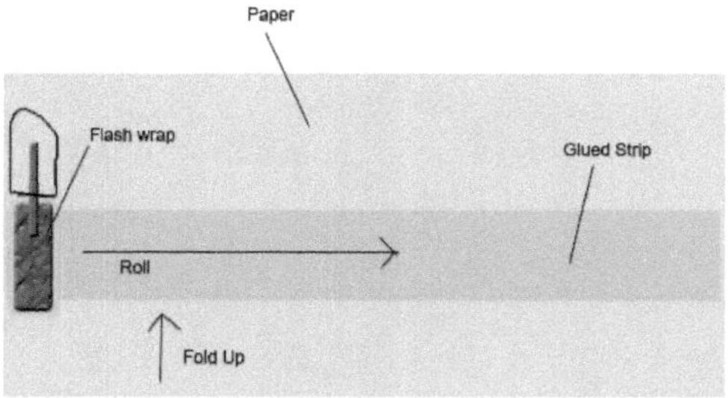

Fig.8.b

3. Using scissors trim away excess paper from the top of the paper tube, allowing the fuse to show. The extra paper is used as a wind block if commercial fuses are not being used for this project.

Final Thoughts

This is an extremely simple pyrotechnic project to make, but as always remember flash powder can be extremely volatile even in the safest of circumstances, always exercise extreme care and caution when using said compounds. Always use protective equipment when dealing with chemical compounds and remember you do not need to pack the flash powder in this project, just ensure it is not very loosely wrapped.

The M-80 Fire Cracker

Once the M-80 fire cracker became available for civilian uses and was marketed as a civilian fire cracker it quickly gained a reputation as the bad boy of fire crackers. This flash powder composition fire cracker packs a lot of punch in a small device. Now some may wonder why I have not included some other pyrotechnic designs such as the ash can or cherry bomb. I found in my research in writing this book, they all follow pretty much the same basic principals, and the M-80 is simply more powerful. With all flash composition projects extreme care and caution must be adhered to at all times, flash powder can be very dangerous if improperly handled or used. Always use protective equipment in all steps of the detailed processes. Some who may be familiar with the M-80's original design will notice some of the materials have been changed, as the original design uses a tin design, this has been changed to avoid injury from flying debris or shrapnel.

Materials Required

	Flash Powder
	Letter/legal sized paper
	½ inch wood dowel
	Drill / X-acto Knife (To cut hole for fuse)
1x	Glue stick
1x	Epoxy / Super glue
1x	3-4 inch Fuse (Commercial grade recommended)

Instructions

1. Using the Paper and glue stick, create a tube that is 2 inch in length, ½ inch inner diameter (use wood dowel) and 1/8 inch tube walls. Allow to dry completely.
2. Using the super glue, stand tube(s) and put 1/8 inch of epoxy/super glue in the bottom of the tube(s) being careful not to get the epoxy/super glue on the inner walls of the tube. Allow to dry completely.

3. ½ way up the tube, cut or drill out a small hole only large enough to fit your fuse in to. (Fig.9.a)

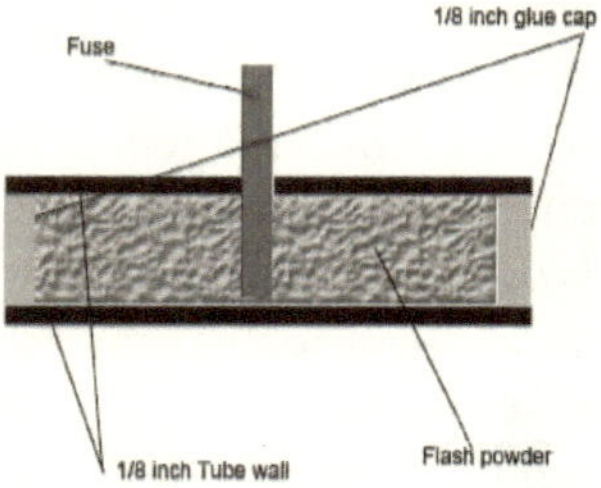

4. After bottom glue end has dried completely fill and carefully pack the flash powder composition into the tube filling up only to the fuse hole. Use extreme caution when packing flash powder and never use metallic items to pack flash powder (only use wood dowel). Once flash powder is packed to fuse hole, insert fuse into hole completely, and continue packing flash powder into tube until 1/8 inch to top of tube.
5. Using super glue, fill the remaining 1/8 inch of top tube with glue, allow to dry completely.

Final Thoughts

The M-80 is relatively easy to make and extremely fun to use, again this can't be stressed enough when using flash powder compositions, extreme care and caution must be utilized when handling, using and especially packing. Children must never handle, use or manufacture flash composite pyrotechnics. And for the love of everything that is good, use common sense when using pyrotechnics. **These pyrotechnics are small explosives, and should never ever be held when lit, as they can and will blow your fingers off.**

Arial Mortars

We all love these wonderful creations of modern pyrotechnics, and for a pyrotechnic project creates many fun and exciting opportunities. The wonderful part about the Arial Mortar is so many variations can be created from the same basic design principals. The system is designed to be fired from a mortar which can either be bought or home made. For the purposes of this project it is highly recommended to use pre fabricated parts from commercial manufacturers as it is safer and provides more reliability. However if the required parts that are called for are unavailable, the parts can be made using tube rolling methods.

Important Warning – Arial Mortar creation is for advanced and knowledgeable users only. Persons creating such devices should have a background in chemistry, physics, and pyrotechnics. Inexperienced persons should never attempt to create Arial Mortars. Children should never be included in any part of the manufacture, ignition or testing of the device. All persons involved must be kept at a safe distance when actual demonstration or test firing is done.

Arial Mortar Physics – Arial mortars work on the basic principal of an explosive base force propels another charge contained within a mortar tubing into the air. Using a delayed ignition the now propelled charge ignites within the sky creating one of many possible pyrotechnic displays. For the purposes of this project we will detail firstly how the base mortar tubing and charge is created. Secondly we will demonstrate how the arial charge is constructed using a basic demonstration. The arial charge can be changed using other types of combinations, however only people with advanced knowledge of how the arial mortar charge works should attempt modification to any of this design.

Parts and chemical compounds – The Arial Mortar calls for use of a lot of very specific parts, and a specific need to high quality, this being said it is highly recommended persons creating Arial Mortars should always buy the parts from a commercial manufacturer. This provides higher reliability and most importantly safety. Home made parts can be created, however advised against, it is impossible to obtain the machine quality of precision. Being the system is a mortar tube design, precision specifically for the tubing is an absolute requirement. Commercial parts can easily be purchased from the internet and most parts (chemicals excluded) are easy to obtain as they don't have restrictions on buying or using them. I have found at the time of writing this book that 3 sites appeared to be very good for commercial fire work supplies, they are: www.skylighter.com, www.pyrodirect.com, www.pyrocreations.com

Materials Required

(Per Arial mortar)

1x Base (Plastic or Wood)

1x Mortar tubing (inner diameter must exact or larger than the arial charges outer diameter)

1x Tubing for arial charge (Must be exact or less than inner diameter of mortar tubing)

1x Small tubing for internal charge

Gunpowder

Flash powder

1x Glue Gun

Drill w/ drill bits

Super Glue

1x Fuse, minimum 5 inch, length varies for time delay.

Cardboard

Card stock paper

Materials Note – The larger the base the more stable the mortar will be, larger bases are recommended for larger and/or more powerful mortars. Fuse length for new/test arial mortar projects should always give the person igniting it more than ample time to get to safety. More time is always better than not enough. It is recommended you design your motars arial charge first, as this will make design of the actual base mortar tube much simpler. However on that note, always ensure before designing a mortar's arial charge the mortars tubing is readily available.

Instructions

Mortar Base

1. Taking the plastic or wooden base, mark the exact center of the base. If possible drill a slight indent the size of the outer diameter of the mortar tube into the base using the drill.
2. If indent was drilled, place the Mortar tubing snugly in the indent. Using glue gun, glue mortar tubing in place and allow to dry completely.
3. Drill a hole large enough for the fuse at the base of the mortar tubing, just above the glue line. (Fig.10.a)

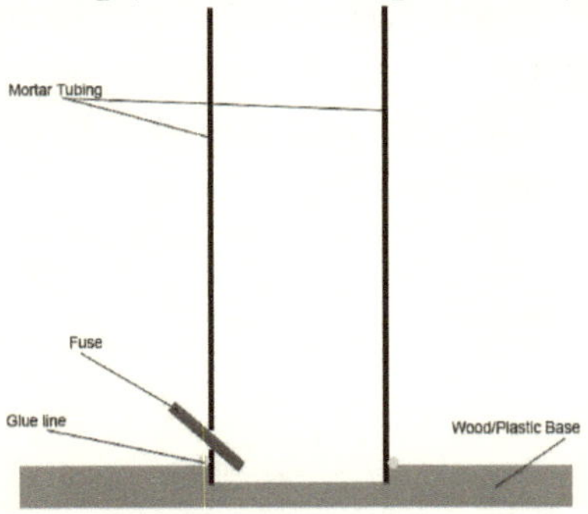

4. Insert fuse into newly drilled hole at base of tube, and secure fuse to base using a drop of super glue. Set aside to fully dry.

Arial Charge

1. Taking your inner tube which shall serve as the arial charge tube, lay it up on a piece of cardstock.
2. Fill 1/8 inch in bottom of tube with super glue, set aside to fully dry.
3. Using the tube rolling technique, create numerous smaller fire cracker tubes ½ the length of inner tube to fit snugly into the inner charge tube.
4. Carefully pack flash powder into small tubes using wood dowel only. Insert fuse into smaller fire crackers.

5. Pack small fire crackers into inner tube to fit as snug as possible. Fig.10.b

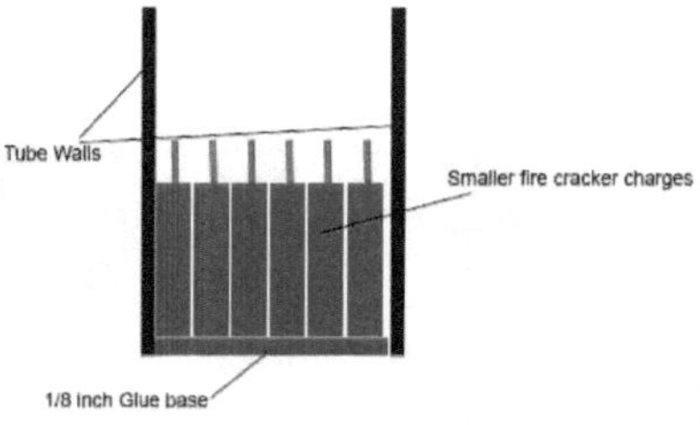

Fig.10.b

6. Ensuring all smaller charge fuses are pointed upright, carefully insert the main delay fuse (length of fuse will determine delay to detonation while in the air. Recommend 3 inches minimum) in to the inner tube and carefully pack flash powder in and around fuse leaving 1/8 inch remaining at top of tube.

7. Using super glue, fill the remaining 1/8 inch at the top of the tube, setting aside to fully dry. (Fig.10.c)

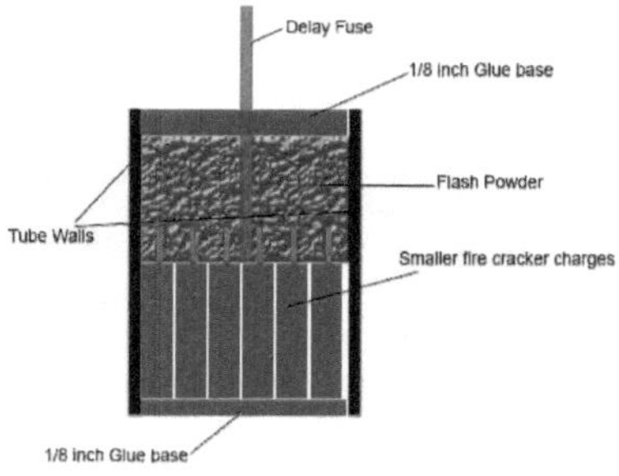

Packing Arial Mortar

1. Using Gunpowder, back the base of the mortar tube, where the ignition fuse is located with gun powder. The amount of gunpowder to be used is determined by the weight, size and desired height the arial charge is to travel up. Leave a little space to add some loose gunpowder at a later step

2. Using card stock, cut 2 circles out of the paper to the size of the inner dimensions of the mortar tube.

3. Taking the arial charge cut out a hole for the fuse in one of the card stock circles, and pull fuse through card stock circle.

4. Put a little loose gunpowder into the mortar tube, on top of the packed powder. Insert the arial charge into the mortar tubing Fuse end down. Carefully pack down arial charge into mortar tube until snug. (Fig.10.d)

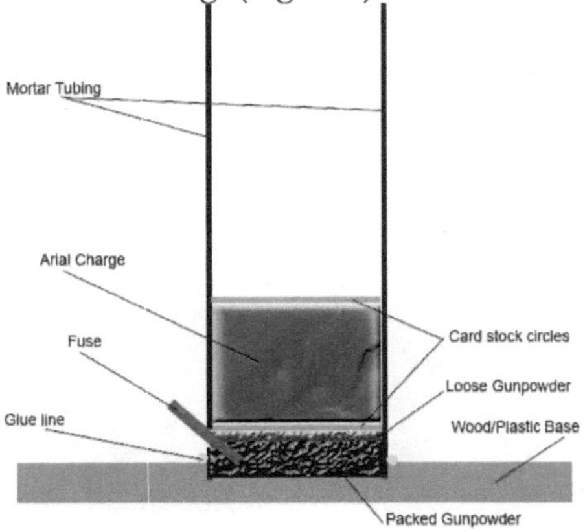

5. Using the second card stock circle place on the top of the now packed arial charge and ensure it fits snugly in the mortar tube.
6. That's it your done! Store Arial Mortar in a safe location away from open flame or heat until ready for testing and use.

Final Thoughts

The described Arial Mortar is a relatively simple design, and will produce a large explosion followed by smaller explosions creating a cracking effect in the sky. Keep in mind this is only a base model to give the creator a foundation for how Arial Mortars work. Experienced users are encouraged to try different variations of arial charges to create different effects. When creating arial mortars it is always advisable to make a couple at a time, and always test them before demonstration. Arial mortars can be extremely dangerous as they contain numerous chemical compounds and the basic nature of the mortar to shoot another explosive charge at high velocity great distances makes this a very dangerous combination. Children should never be included in the creation, ignition, or testing of arial mortars. All persons should remain at a safe distance when firing for both demonstration and testing. A remote detonator or very long delay fuse is recommended for the testing of arial mortars. Never look in to, or point a loaded mortar at anyone/anything. Always use proper protective equipment for the process of making or using arial mortars.

Roman Candles

Roman candles are a classic and favorite firework for all ages, These tubes of 8 or 12 shot explosive pyrotechnic demonstration are sure to widen the eye and have everyone looking to the sky. So then why no Roman candle project? Well the answer is simple. Upon preparing to write the method of creation for roman candles, I deemed it was too complex and had too many variables for which something could go wrong. It is a long and pain staking process to produce even a single roman candle tube and ultimately just cheaper, better and more reliable to buy them from a manufacturer. I made an entry in the book to show that no this classic was not forgotten, but decidedly left out for the reasons mentioned above.

Military Grade Smoke Bombs

Smoke Bombs are not only fun but a great diversion. Igniting one of these will release large amounts of thick white smoke into the surrounding area. This mixture is relatively simple and easy to make and contains no gunpowder or flash powder to create.

Materials Required

1x	Hotplate
1x	Tube
1x	Plastic tub/jar
1x	Fuse 4+ inch in length
	Saltpeter
	Sugar
	Mixing pot (use an old pot)
	Wood spoon

Instructions

The chemical breakdown for this mixture is as follows:

60%	Saltpeter
40%	Sugar

1. Combine Saltpeter and sugar compounds together in plastic tub/jar and mix together thoroughly using wood spoon.
2. Pour saltpeter and sugar mixture into mixing pot, and heat on a low to medium heat on hot plate. This is to be done outdoors only, as there is a high risk that the mixture could ignite.
3. While heating saltpeter and sugar mixture ensure you are stirring the mixture thoroughly using the wooden spoon until the mixture starts to caramelize into a thick syrup.
4. After all remaining powder has been absorbed and converted into the now sugar syrup composition, remove from hot plate.

5. Quickly, while the syrup is still in a liquid state, pack the syrup mixture into the tube and insert a fuse into mixture at the end of the tube. Set aside and allow to fully dry.

Final Thoughts

Smoke bombs are great fun, and very easy to make. When making smoke bombs always ensure it is done outdoors in case of accidental ignition you will not be smoked out of your working area. In the event you wish to make different colored smoke bombs ie – Red, Blue, Green you can add additional chemicals to the mixture to achieve the desired color effect, this is detailed later on in this section.

Chemical Color Chart

This topic leads in from the smoke bomb project as this chart below provides the chemical mixtures to produce different types of colors using chemical reactions. Although it is rumored that adding simple food coloring to the chemical mixtures it is not advised as this can produce un expected results from the various chemical compositions. This chart can also be used to produce different desired pyrotechnic effects such as different colored explosions and trails for fire crackers and arial mortars.

	Black	**White**
1	Magnesium powder – 19% Hexachloroethane – 60% Napthalene – 21%	Potassium chlorate – 44% Sulfur flour – 15% Zinc dust – 40% Sodium bicarbonate – 1%
2	Magnesium powder – 20% Hexachloroethane – 60% Napthalene – 20%	Zinc dust – 66.37% Hexachloroethane – 33.33%
3	Hexachloroethane – 55.80% Alpha Naphol – 14% Athracene – 4.60% Aluminum powder – 9.30% Smokeless powder – 14% Naphthalene – 2.30%	Zinc dust – 28% Zinc oxide – 22% Hexachloroethane – 50%
4	Black powder FFF – 50% Potassium nitrate – 10% Coal tar – 20% Powdered charcoal – 15% Paraffin – 5%	

<table>
<tr><th></th><th>Yellow</th><th>Green</th><th>Red</th></tr>
<tr><td>1</td><td>Potassium chlorate – 25%
Paranitraniline – 50%
Lactrose – 25%</td><td>Potassium nitrate – 20
Red arsenic – 20
Sulfur flour – 20
Antimony sulfide – 20
Black powder FFF – 20</td><td>Potassium chlorate – 20%
Lactose – 20%
Paranitraniline red – 60%</td></tr>
<tr><td>2</td><td>Potassium chlorate – 30%
Naphthalene azodimethyl anline – 50%
Powdered sugar – 20%</td><td></td><td>Potassium chlorate – 26%
Diethylaminorosindone – 48%
Powdered sugar – 26%</td></tr>
<tr><td>3</td><td>Potassium chlorate – 21.40%
Naphthalene azodimethylanline – 2.70%
Auramine – 38%
Sodium biocarbonate – 28.50%
Sulfur flour – 9.40%</td><td></td><td>Potassium chlorate – 27.40%
Methylaminoanthraquinone – 42.50%
Sodium bicarbonate – 19.50%
Sulfur flour – 10.60%</td></tr>
<tr><td>4</td><td></td><td></td><td>Potassium pechlorate – 25%
Antimony sulfide – 20%
Rhodamine red – 50%
Dextrin – 5%</td></tr>
</table>

Section 3

Outdoor Shelters, Trenches, Tree top Platforms, Zip lines, and Bridges

Trenches and Covered Positions

Every military in the world uses these techniques, and for a good reason, trenches provide invaluable protection from elements and opposition. These make shift positions can be made virtually anywhere there is solid ground and have numerous designs, variable additions, and other great elements making these a great project for the outdoors person. Be it for Shelter or cover for a paint ball game, trenches are simple inexpensive and above all fun to use. In this section we will cover the basics of trenches and provide some possible designs for them.

The Basics of Trenches

With trench digging/design there is no set rules for how they are designed, so we will recommend the base line as specified by the US military. These specifications are more guidelines rather than set rules, all the variables can be modified for your own specific needs/designs.

- Trenches are generally designed to be arm pit height in depth, this allows the person within the trench to be standing upright fully with only there head and arms visible, this height also allows for easy cover by simply crouching down.
- Trenches are generally designed to be 4-5 foot in path diameter, the smaller of a passage way the less chance of the trench being noticed. The larger the trench is dug out, the more obvious it is. Smaller is better, however ensure you have enough room to actively move around without being pressed up against the trench side walls.
- Re-enforce permanent trenches using wood planks as the trench wall sides. (Will be diagramed later)
- Re-enforce all over head covers, remember when building anything that provides over head cover it is always better to edge on the side of caution than have the roof/cover come down and bury you inside.
- Don't get lazy in your design / Don't cut corners. Be realistic, digging holes is tedious and pain staking at times. Trenches require you to dig holes, so if you don't like digging, it is probably better not to do trenches at all, cutting corners in trench digging/re-enforcement can prove dangerous and even fatal at

times. Remember, if you are going to do it, do it right the first time. Safety is paramount in all projects in this book. Trenches although simple in design are no different than any other project detailed within this book, Safety first!

Figure 11.a details a cut away view of a standard trench design.

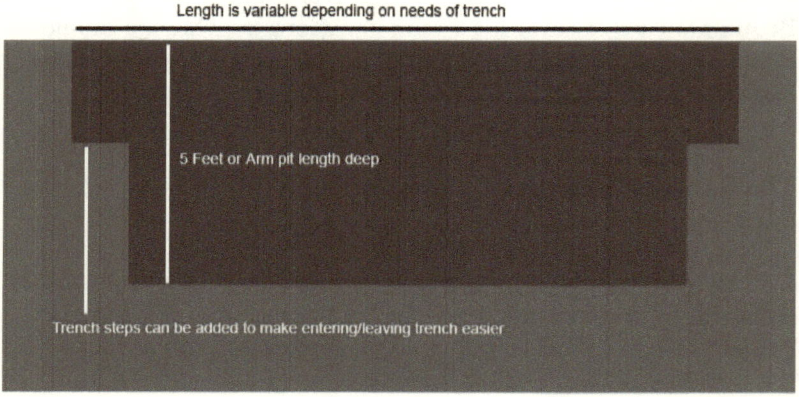

Length is variable depending on needs of trench
5 Feet or Arm pit length deep
Trench steps can be added to make entering/leaving trench easier

Fig.11.a

Trench Walls

Trench walls are needed for permanent trench positions, trench walls are designed very simply, but do require resources such as wood and a hammer (standard and sledge). The design for trench walls is very basic; you ensure the dirt wall to be re-enforced is as flat as possible (no major dirt, rocks or roots sticking out into the trench). Using 2x4 planks of wood, you will sink posts into the ground at least 2 feet deep into the trench ground, roughly 3 inches away from dirt trench wall (just enough to fit the wall boards in). Posts are required every 5-8 feet in distance, the closer together to more strength the posts will have. Sink wall posts into ground using a sledge hammer or other heavy object, posts must be secure and stable in ground. Following your posts, you will then use 2x6/2x8 wood boards to line the walls with a wooden wall. (it is ideal to use pre cut wood, however natural branches can be substituted and even preferred at times to get a more of a outdoor feel to your trench) Wall boards are then nailed or tied into place. After wooden walls are secured, fill remaining gap between wooden walls and dirt wall with dirt. See Fig.11.b for diagram

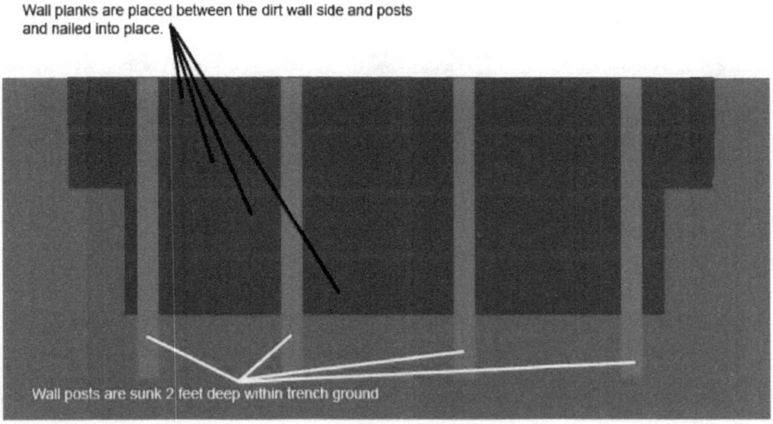
Wall planks are placed between the dirt wall side and posts and nailed into place.
Wall posts are sunk 2 feet deep within trench ground

Fig.11.b

Trench Flooring

Trench flooring although not required can make poor weather conditions much more bearable and less messy. Also it ensures a flat ground surface; this will assist in preventing injury from tripping on rocks, roots or clumps of dirt. The design of flooring is also very simple, it uses 2x4 boards as "lift" from the ground (allows for a small amount of space between the dirt ground and the wooden flooring platform) and 2x4 boards as the actual flooring. Small spacing should be given between each board as this allows for free flow of dirt and water to sift below the floor boards. See Fig.11.c. Again there is no perfect design, these are basics which are meant to serve as a foundation of understanding, you can always modify or change these details to better suit your needs.

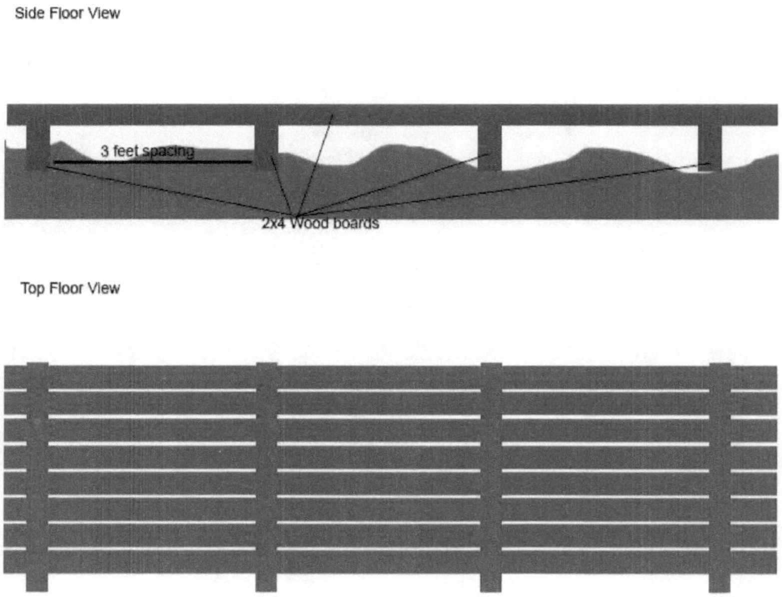

Fig.11.c

Covered Trenches / Areas

Creating Covered trenches follows the same basic foundation work as a standard trench with the following exceptions:

- Underground trenches are deeper than standard trenches, standard trenches are in general 5 feet in depth, covered trenches require 8-10 feet in depth as they must provide ample support for overhead beams and also provide enough room for persons to stand upright within trench.
- Covered trenches are larger than standard trenches, being they will be covered and protected; covered trenches are generally made larger than standard trenches this is done to provide storage or shelter, and these can be used for equipment storage, sleeping quarters, or any other use.
- Covered trenches can be dangerous, as they will be providing shelter and will have overhead support beams to create a natural roof; there is always the possibility of a cave in. This being said is it extremely important to build covered trenches with care and caution, always ensure the beams being used for the roof will handle the load placed on top of it.

- Routinely check the condition of the support beams. Immediately fix any found problems with the roof.

Covered trenches are designed usually square, they will use support beams which in this design will be no lesser than 4x4 beams. (6x6 recommended) Beams will sit on a platform which is dug out 3 feet from the actual trench and 2-3 feet deep from ground level (See Fig.11.d), this is done to provide ample support for the load which will be placed on top of the beams from the dirt roof. After the trench design is dug out and support shelves defined, place in sequence the support beams within the dirt shelves and place a waterproofing tarp or plastic cover over top of the support beams, and top with dirt until level with surrounding ground. Pack the dirt down after completion.

Cut away view of covered trench

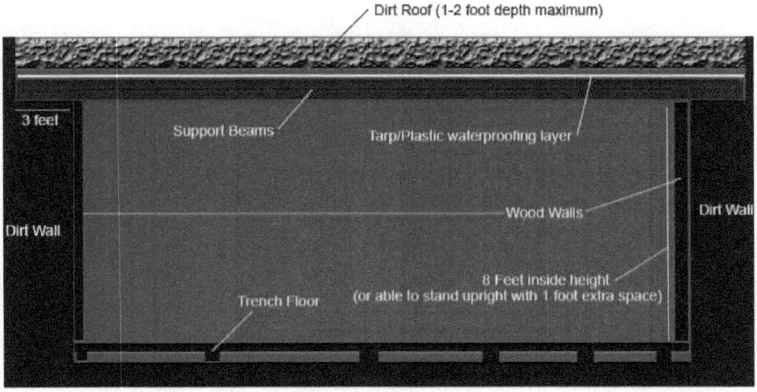

Fig.11.d

Covered trench entry ways can be designed either off of a standard trench or have its own entry, usually consisting of a foxhole going to trench ground level and a ladder to access from ground level. The door frame will use support beams to provide ample support (also allows for a door to added) Door support beams will be sunk 1 foot deep on trench ground level. This is done to add support for both trench wall and over head support. See Fig.11.e

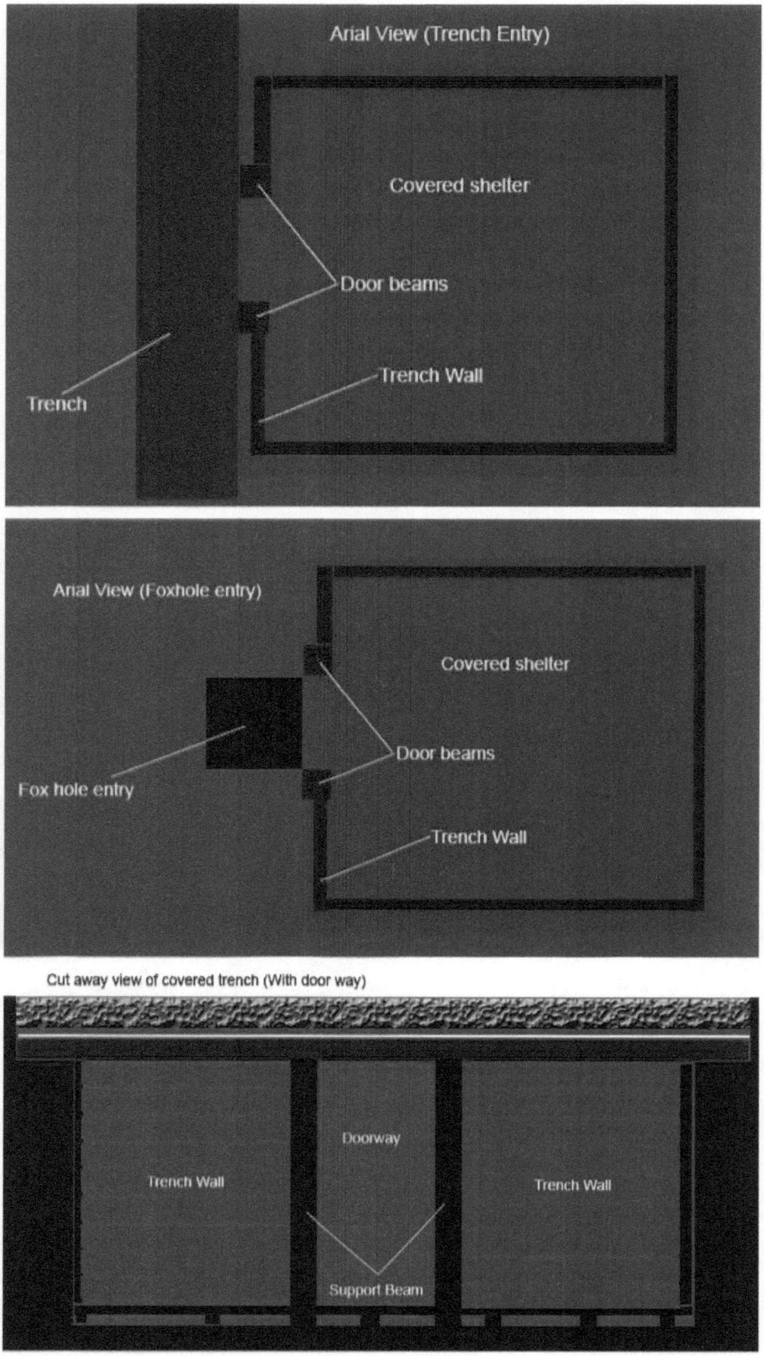
Arial View (Trench Entry)
Covered shelter
Door beams
Trench Wall
Trench
Arial View (Foxhole entry)
Covered shelter
Door beams
Fox hole entry
Trench Wall
Cut away view of covered trench (With door way)
Doorway
Trench Wall
Trench Wall
Support Beam

Fig.11.e

Observation positions are used in more complex series of trenches/underground bases. These consist of a covered trench and a small window used for observation or shooting. These covered trenches are used on hillsides as the window side requires a graded ground level to be effective. Variations are possible, however a hillside is best recommended for covered observation trench positions. The only change to modification of a covered trench is the window well; the window will consist of support beam construction for support. It is best recommended the keep the observation windows narrow in height as this reduces the chance of them being spotted. Windows are situated near the top of the covered trench close to the roof support beams. See Fig.11.f

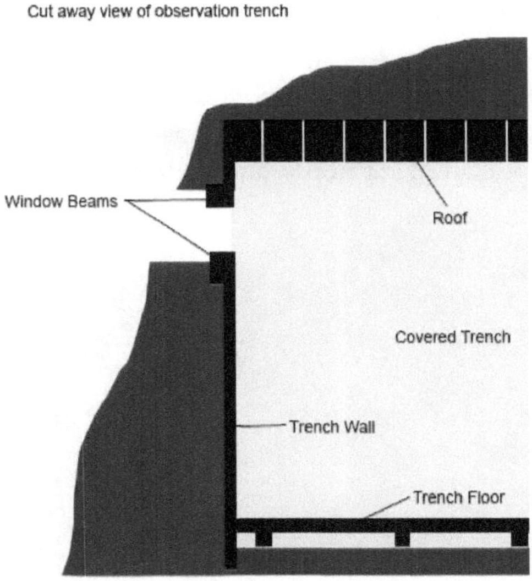

Fig.11.f

Trench and Covered Trench Design Theory.

In this section we will discuss various design applications for trench positions. The basic theory of trench design can be complex at times, this being the variables on your needs for the trench post. Depending on how secure you need areas to be will determine how your trench layout is designed. Generally speaking, the more secure your area needs to be the farther away from the entry way it will be. You may have a desire to create a complex system of covered trench tunnels, or simply a trench fighting position for quick cover. Natural surrounding area also plays a large part in your trench design, the more natural cover you have the harder an open or uncovered trench will be spotted or found, for larger open areas covered trenches are more suitable as they provide the basic camouflage of ground cover. The following diagrams are designed to give a rough idea of some basic trench designs. Again, these designs can be modified to best suit your needs, and is encouraged!

Sample Trench Diagrams

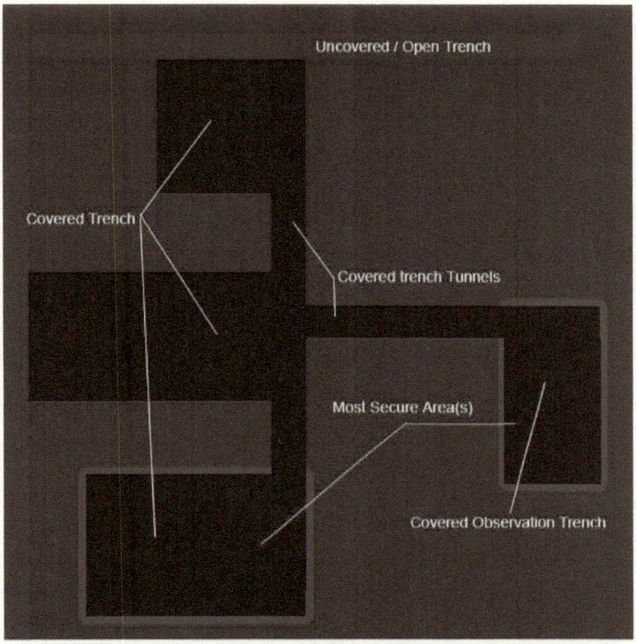

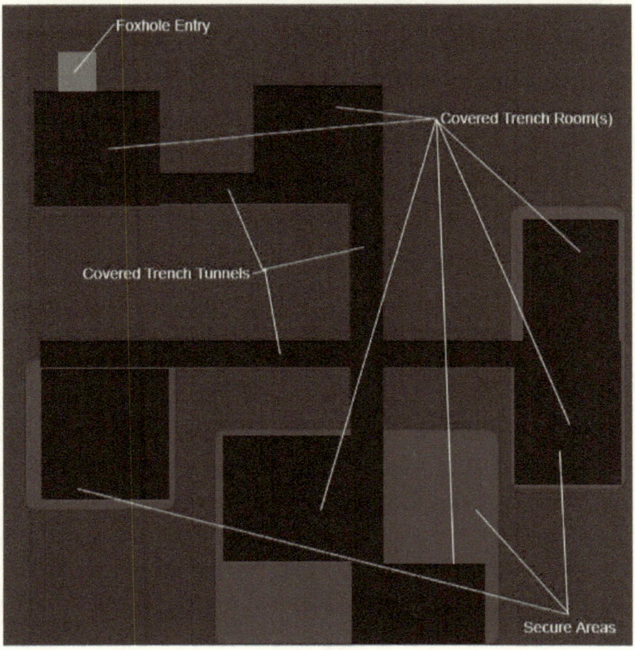

Trench Ventilation

With more complex trench designs, in specific trench designs that contain numerous covered areas, or lengthy tunnel systems, ventilation shafts are required. This is done by creating an open shaft from the covered area to the ground level, I recommend using 1-2 inch plywood to create the ventilation shafts. These shafts can either be placed within the structure of the roof or sideways from ground level to the wall side of the covered shelter. Regardless of which approach you decide upon, ventilation shafts are a absolute must for safety. Ventilation shafts should be roughly 6-8 inches in diameter to provide proper circulation of air. Ventilation shafts must be checked routinely to ensure there are no blockages which would restrict proper air flow within the covered areas. Ventilation shafts and observation windows not only help provide air circulation through the trench area, but also double as sources of light.

Trench Lighting

The best and most natural light source within a covered trench is the sun itself, however being an underground structure this obviously poses its own problems. Using ventilation shafts and observation windows helps immensely with light within covered trenches however night use and other variables make the sun an unreliable source of light. We recommend using portable lights or glow stick to illuminate the covered trenches and tunnels. Fire is never to be used as a source of light in a trench, as it poses a fire and smoke hazard being within a covered area which uses wooden supports to hold its self up and together.

Ensure trench tunnels and covered areas as well illuminated to avoid possible trip hazards. Running around in dark tunnels or areas is never advisable.

Other Trench Considerations and Concerns

Covered trenches by nature are perfect shelters. This being said it is not uncommon that our animal counter parts would find these an ideal place to make a home for themselves and their furry family. Before using trenches and coverings always clear them first by going through with a light source and ensure no animals have made a nest in the covered areas. If they are unwilling to leave on their own you will have to remove of them in a humane method. One method which works effectively is to use a smoke bomb (detailed in the pyrotechnic section) to clear the trenches of animals. No creature will willingly remain in an area which is filled with noxious smoke, and will naturally leave to find better or more suitable shelter for themselves and their family. (Always allow smoke to fully clear trenches and covered areas before using!)

When attempting to remove any wildlife from your trenches or covered areas, always maintain caution, wild animals can be very unpredictable. Never corner an animal and always allow them free passage away from yourselves. Animals will in general avoid areas which are marked by human scent, so the more often your covered trenches are used the better. Animals will pick up on the fact it is a human dwelling, and will usually avoid it. For more troublesome animals which refuse to leave using other methods you should consider calling a professional to have the animals removed. Again, wild life can be very unpredictable and they will defend what they perceive as there space. Doors can be added to covered trench areas to deter animals from making a home of your covered trench. Doors also help to hold in heat in winter conditions.

Camp Shelters

In this section we will discuss other various forms of shelters mainly used for camps. These types of shelter usually consist of natural items such as branches, leaves etc, allowing them to double as natural camouflage. Camp shelters usually are not designed to be permanent or long term shelters. For long term shelters it is best to build using solid materials and re-enforced with nails, screws, or rope to reliably hold the structure together.

Bough Shelters

Bough shelters are simply the use of a tree branch either fallen or bend drawn down towards the ground to provide a basic roof and wind shelter. Bough shelters are convenient and easy to make however should not be used frequently as there condition and stability can change by the day. See Fig.12.a

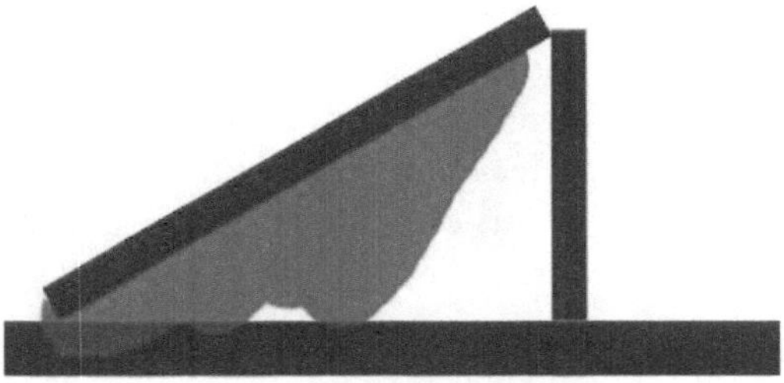

Fig.12.a

Natural / Artificial Hollow Shelters

Natural or artificial hollow shelters are similar to covered trenches however they are designed to be cozy in size, and are primarily used to sleep and gain protection from the environmental elements. By either finding a natural hollow in the ground or digging one out, you use thick branches to layer over top of the hollow to create a basic hole in the ground, followed by layering leaves and other debris over the branch frame. This provides basic protection from the wind and rain. Take note however to be cautious on water drainage, otherwise you may find yourself lying in a puddle of water. See Fig.12.b

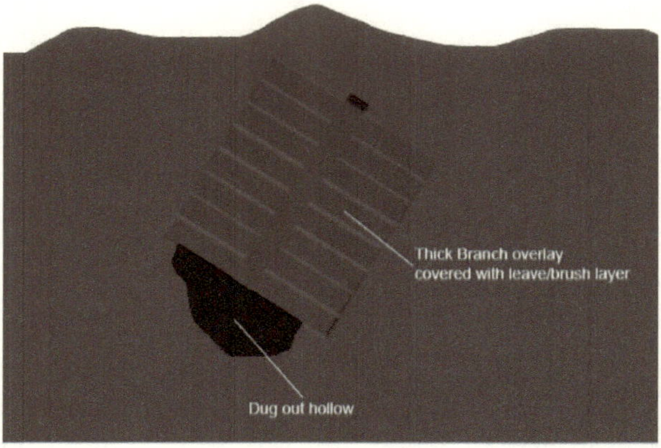

Fig.12.b

Open Lean-To Shelter

The open lean-to shelter is a good temporary shelter if you have some time to make it, the shelter basics consist of two supports which hold up a a back drop of branches to provide a base to layer leaves and debris against to create an effective shelter against the wind and light rains. The two supporting posts or branches can be either thick branches sunk into the ground or trees. Using rope or cord fashioned from tree bark you secure the branches and sloped base using the rope, followed by layering leaves and other debris against the sloped side to create the cover. See Fig. 12.c

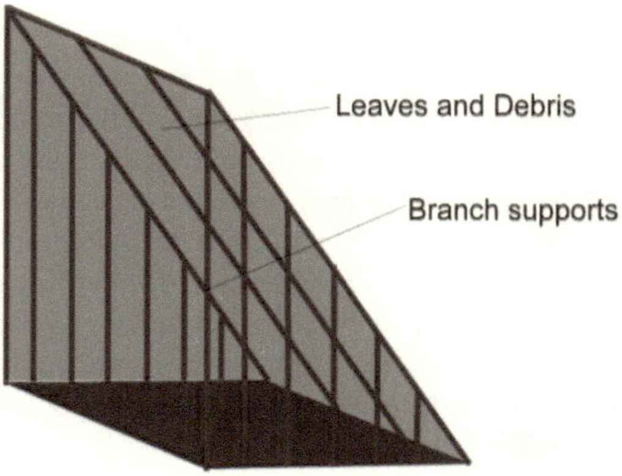

Fig.12.c

Tarp Shelters

Tarp shelters are quick and easy to make and provide an effective temporary shelter from the natural elements. The tarp shelter is very similar in design to older model tents, which use support poles, and a guide wire to hold the tarp up and in place. See Fig.12.d

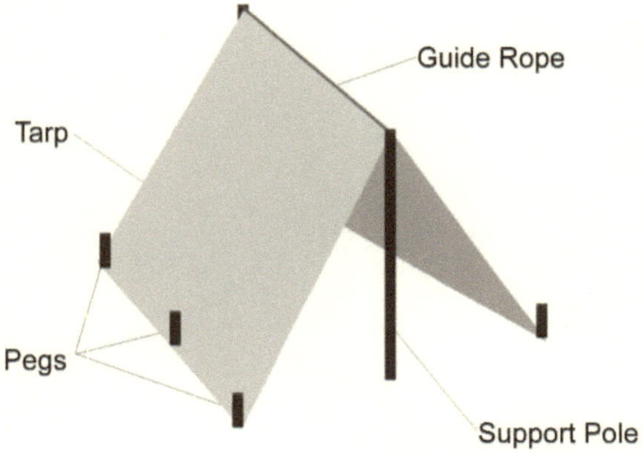

Fig.12.d

Tree Top Platforms / Tree Forts

Every kid under the sun loves tree forts; there is just something about being above the rest of the world that can't be beat. This section will cover some of the basics to designing a successful tree top platform and/or fort. These are guidelines which can be modified to best suit your needs.

Tree top platform/fort safety is vital to ensure people who use the platform remain safe from fall hazards. As always the safety for any project is upon the end users liability to ensure anything they build is safe and secure. Being construction of a tree top platform is above ground level, it is unadvised children be involved in the construction of these projects. All supporting beams must be secured to tree bases/trunks using bolts. Use of bolts and screws for tree top platforms is recommended for any aspect which requires the frame/foundations to be secure, screws and bolts are threaded leaving less chance they will come separated with time. Nails should only be used for non structural aspects such as wall siding or roofs. Never build the platforms too high on the trees, the higher you go on a tree the less support the trees center trunk has to offer. Although we would all love to make a tree top society like in the Swiss family Robinson, it's simply not feasible, nor is it advisable! So don't try to build your platforms too high.

This next section will discuss various methods to securing the frames to trees. There are numerous methods to doing this, we will cover the basics. As treetop platforms and forts can vary greatly in design and structural development I will be covering only the main aspects as I could write a whole book on this topic alone. If you do not have experience in the basics of construction it is advisable to seek professional advice on the design and structural support system to be used for a project such as this.

There is never an excuse for cutting corners, or not obtaining advice for situations where you may not be knowledgeable. Searching the internet will yield numerous results in detailed plans for tree houses. It is advisable to either purchase professional plans, or have someone with experience create the plans. Always add Guard rails and walls to avoid fall hazards. Again safety is paramount; I really do not want to be getting hate mail because some random person decided to build their kid a tree house and the thing collapsed on them injuring their child. These projects are provided for fun, so ensure safety is followed at all times!

Single Tree Support

The single tree support is in general most reliable as it does not require additional supports from surrounding trees or posts in the ground. Although if possible using additional post supports for the platform end which is not supported by the trees trunk is ideal, it may not be possible given considerations to surrounding terrain or many other aspects. The Single tree support system is fairly straight forward, the base support beam is designed like a T, followed with 2 other boards cut with ends angled at 45 degrees to attach to base and support beam to provide additional support to main support beam. This is fastened to the trees center trunk using bolts. This assures secure support to the trees trunk while providing ample support for both ends of the platforms support beams. You may also wish to tie the main platform support beam to the tree using rope to provide additional support. See Fig.13.a

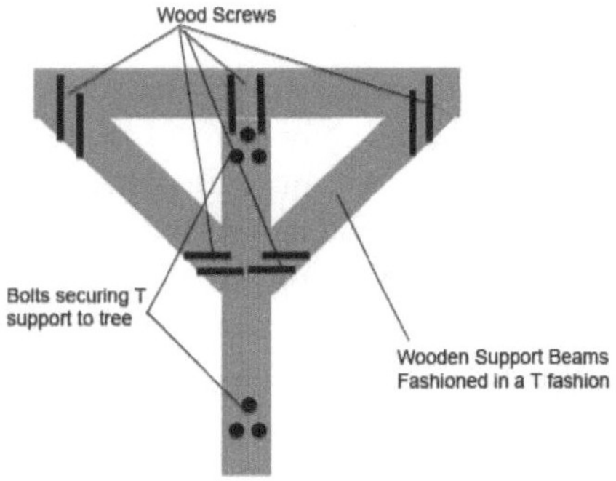

Fig.13.a

T Support Frame Attached to Tree Trunk

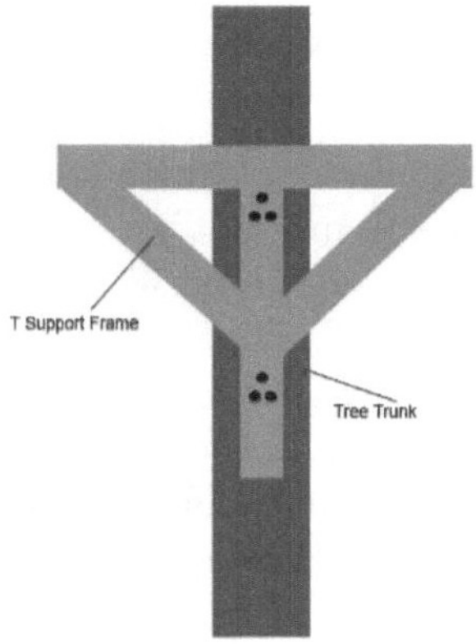

Fig.13.a.1

Main Platform

Building the main platform can be argued to be the trickiest portion of this design as the central T support beam is generally advised to have in place before putting the central platform in place. The platform is built using a framed area, using wooden beams as underlying supports for the floor boards. The edge furthest from the tree requires further support beams which will tie back into the trees trunk to add support for the alternate side of the platform. For all support beams you must use bolts. To tie supports into the trees trunk you must use Long Threaded Bolts to tie securely into the trunk. See Fig.13.b

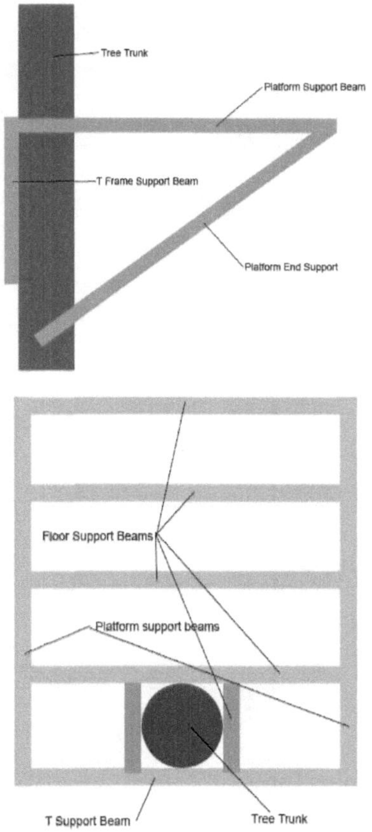

Fig.13.b

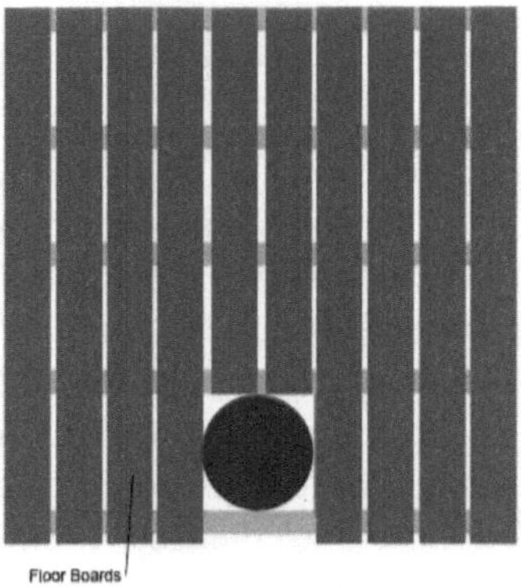

Fig.13.b (continued)

Dual Tree Support

Using 2 trees for the supporting system for a platform is easier yet more complex than a single tree design. It is easier for the factors T support framing is not required, less of a load is placed on a single tree, and in general construction is simpler than a single tree design. However with any design there are draw backs as well. Using 2 trees for supports adds more variables to the support equation. Remember, as trees grow older with time they expand, and grow larger, trees do not grow at the same pace as one another and different types of trees also grow at different rates of speed. These are all variables which must be considered when choosing your trees which will be the supports for your platforms frame.

As with any project where construction or building is required, it is required to routinely check the finished item to ensure it is safe and stable. Always ensure support beams are well anchored to the supporting trunks/posts. If they become unsafe it is time to either fix the support system by building a new one in place, or to remove it in whole. It is never worth risking the safety of people due to times damages on any project. It is better to just start fresh than to be breaking bones or even causing death from a fall hazard.

The construction of the Dual tree platform system is very close to the basic design of the Single tree design, however with a couple exceptions. As mentioned the T support frame is no longer required, this in place will be replaced with a Cross beam connected to the two trees, and support beams run out from the sides of the trees. See Fig.13.c

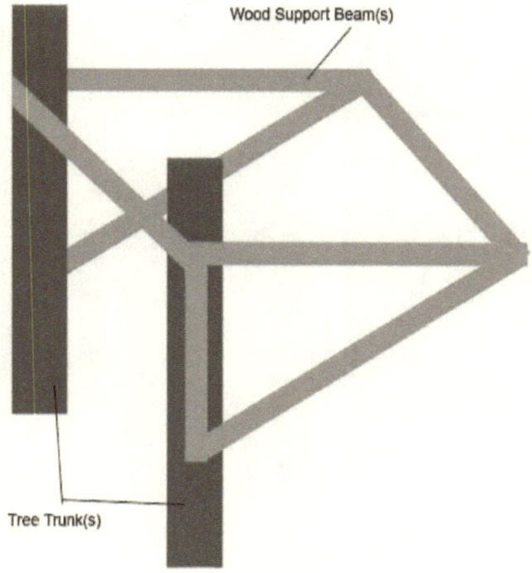

Fig.13.c

Dual Tree Main Platform

Not much changes with the main platform from the single tree design; it is still basically the same design with a slight modification to accommodate the 2 tree trunks instead of the single one. See Fig.13.d

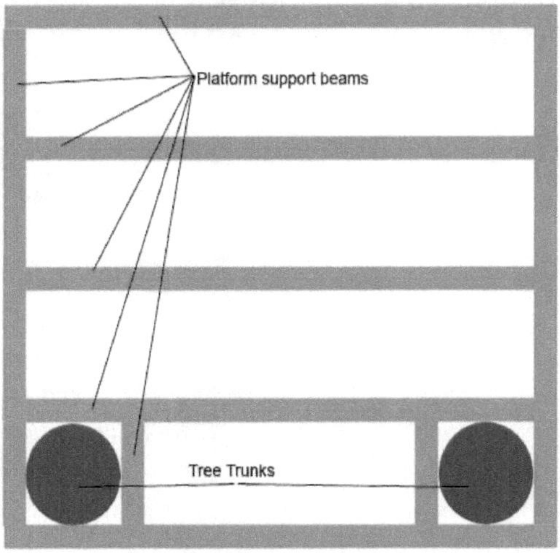

Fig.13.d

The Floor boards are placed on the same way they are for the single tree platform; nail them to the floor supporting beams to create a crisscross pattern. See Fig.13.e

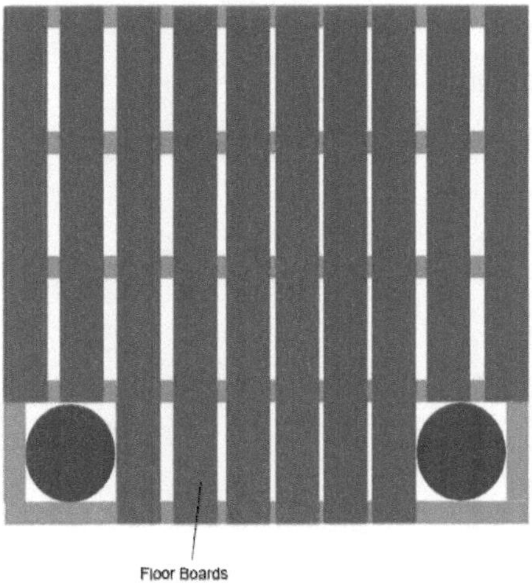

Fig.13.e

Tree Top Platform Considerations and Concerns

As mentioned at the beginning of this section, these are the basics to creating a tree top platform or fort. Design specifications can and will vary from design to design. Walls, Guard Rails and Roof's can also be added (Guard rails if not walls should be added to all platforms for safety). Basic construction knowledge is required to build a proper platform, and should not be attempted by persons who do not have experience in dealing with construction. Access to the platforms can be from numerous methods; however we recommend using a ladder, be it solid or rope.

Children should never be charged with assisting in the construction of the platforms due to safety risks such as fall hazards or injury from the materials or tools themselves. Anyone involved in constructing above ground platforms, tree or otherwise, should always use fall protection such as a safety harness. Platforms should be routinely checked for stability and safety, if the platform becomes unsafe for use, it should be fixed or taken down immediately. Platforms which use trees as support will become unstable in time as the tree grows, so it is vital they be routinely checked!

For those who are serious about building a top notch tree top platform or tree house, I recommend you do some internet surfing and find some blue prints to your liking, however like anything found on the internet ensure it is from a reputable source. Always use common sense, that 100 year old maple tree might seem like an ideal tree to build off of, however it may not be safe, it could have root rot or many other things which could turn this fun project into a disaster. Trees are not magical supporting beams from the earth; they have their limits as to how much stress and weight can be placed on them before they give way. If you think a tree may be too weak to build off of, chances are it probably is.

Have fun with these projects, majority of these projects with the exception of certain ones which specifically advise you not to deviate or substitute items in the project can be modified to better suit your desires. This being said, have fun in the designs and be creative, however keep in mind the basic principles of the design to ensure you will not over stress the supporting trees or other items.

Building a Zip line

Zip lines are fun for all ages; there is something about soaring down a rope on a pulley system that just can't be beat. Zip lines are fun and very easy to build with very little required tools or experience to create. In this section we will discuss how to build your very own zip line.

Zip line design is relatively simple, using a rope or cable you attach the two ends to secure anchors (tree, post, etc..) The starting point is always of a higher level, however it is not too high where excessive speeds are obtained, we recommend a 20 degree angle. Although Zip lines are in general very strong and stable, creating excessively long lines can cause problems such as getting stuck in the middle of the line. Rope in specific causes this issue more so than steel cable as rope tends to sag with weight applied to it. For the purposes of this project we will recommend use of a steel cable to avoid sagging of the line when in use.

In the example given below we will be using steel cable for the line, a pulley, a bar for handles, and a tree top platform for the starting point. However, variations are around in which other materials can be used, however we recommend use of Steel cable and pulleys which are appropriated rated for 200 lbs of weight or higher. Natural hills or other things can be used instead of a tree top platform instead as the starting point.

Firstly you need a starting point. This is generally done by a hill side or tree top platform. Using the cable or rope, you secure the starting end to the support beam (in this example a tree's trunk). Following the attachment of the start of the line, you then thread the Pulley and bar system through the cable. You then take the second end (which will be the end point) and secure it to another lower base supporting beam (another tree) and ensure the cable/rope is pulled very tightly to ensure as little sagging will occur as possible when in use. We recommend adding a second smaller rope or line to the actual pulley system so you can easily bring the system back to the starting point. If you do not attach the secondary rope to the pulley it can be difficult to reset the system due to the height of the starting point. See Fig.14.* for Zip line diagram.

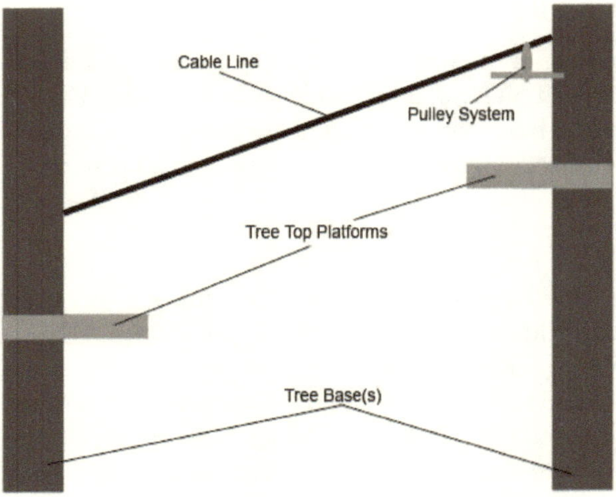

Fig.14.a – Overview of Zip Line

Making the Pulley Handle Bar

The pulley handle bar system is most likely the most complex part of this project as pulleys differ in design and construction. This being said there is no set method to creating the pulley handle bar, however if possible we recommend using a steel bar or bicycle handle bars for the bar, connecting the handle bars to the pulley is the trickiest part, if possible and using all steel construction it is best to weld them together as this will ensure they are safe, secure and wont fail when in use. If you are unable to weld the handle bars, another method is to use a steel bar which is of suitable length for a handle bar and insert the bar through the load end of the pulley and using a drill, drill 2 holes large enough to fit a nut and bold on each side of the pulley to hold the bar in place. Regardless of the method you decide upon, always ensure the pulley handle bar system can and will support the weight by testing it out at ground level **before connecting to zip line cable**. See Fig.14.b

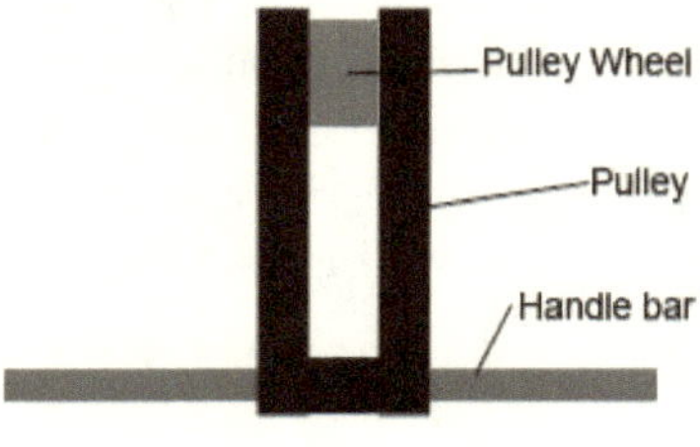

Fig.14.b – Pulley Handlebar System

Bridges

Bridges play a vital role in our society and there uses are very apparent. The desire to build bridges comes from the basic principle of having to cross a large span or drop easily and safely. Whether it's a river, open hole or valley. Bridges serve as an easy and effective way to get from one side to another without having to go around the obstacle.

Construction of bridges is fairly straight forward and almost all bridges follow the same basic requirements of requiring 2 sides to anchor the bridge ends to, Foundation or support for both ends, and a solid construction for the bridge itself. Bridges can be built using many various types of materials be it steel or wood. In this section we will cover the basic foundations of bridge building and explain how to build the simpler designs of bridges. Complex bridges such as suspension and cantilever should not be attempted by novice bridge builders and left to actual bridge engineers due to the complex nature of their design.

Never attempt to build a bridge that has a very large span between two sides. Never build bridges over extremely deep drops. Safety is paramount with all projects in this book; however when dealing with heights extra caution and care must always be taken. Fall hazards can and will present themselves through the duration of building such items as bridges and arial platforms. Using fall protection while constructing such items is mandatory.

In this section we are going to cover the basics of three type of bridges, Beam, Rope and Draw Bridge. Both follow the same basic design for the physical bridge platform; however both utilize different methods of securing them to the ground/end points.

Bridge Basics

When designing a bridge, location and placement of the bridge is vital to its success. In general it is always advised to choose the shortest distance available between the two sides. This allows for construction of a shorter and therefore stronger bridge. Ensuring the bridge ends are anchored and properly supported is also a critical concern for bridge building. Bridge ends should be placed on flat dry land, water and other natural hazards will cause the bridge to become unstable. Never build the bridge ends too close to the drop edge. If your building a bridge across a river or valley, it is important to remember although when initial design of the bridge the drop edge may be stable now, however in time it may become unstable by many various aspects such as erosion caused by the constant movement of water against it, or simply the movement of the ground itself. Always build giving as much of a ground platform as possible (Allow 10-20 feet minimum of bridge surface on ground level before drop edge on each side). With all constructed projects you must routinely check the bridge for safety, if supporting beams show signs of rot, stress or splintering. They must either be removed or replaced as soon as possible to avoid injury. Always use rail guards on ALL bridges. There is no exception or excuse to not implement a rail on both sides of the bridge. If you are going to spend the time to build a bridge, spend that little bit extra time to ensure safety of its users. The writer of this book will not be held liable for your failure to follow safety precautions.

Beam Bridges

Beam bridges are most likely the simplest and safest of the bridges detailed in this section as the bridge will always remain stationary. The basic design of this bridge consists of 2 supporting beams which will act as the frame for the rest of the bridge. And wood planks to serve to needs of the bridge walkway itself. It is important to use beams which are suitable for the bridges weight load. For our bridge design we will recommend 6x6 beams. Larger beams are required for longer span bridges.

Depending on the terrain where the bridge is to be build will determine your needs for support and anchoring. Beam bridges are considered static (ie – no movement). This being said it is not necessarily required to anchor the bridge to the ground, however it is always recommended. Weather and other natural events can cause the bridge although static to move or be jolted about. This is especially true for people who live in areas where earth quakes, tornados, flooding and other natural disasters are common.

Large span bridges may require numerous beams to be connected. Using wood this can be done relatively easily with safety being kept in mind at all times, however it is critical to not over stretch your bridges supporting beams, do not attach too many sections of beam. The more connections used to connect the supporting beams the more strain is placed on them all, as more stress is added to the bridges support frame the less of a load it can safely handle. This being said I do not want to hear about someone trying to build a bridge across extremely large gaps or openings. So no trying to bridge across something ridiculous like the Grand Canyon! Leave that to the professionals. Fig.15.a details the basic design of a beam bridge.

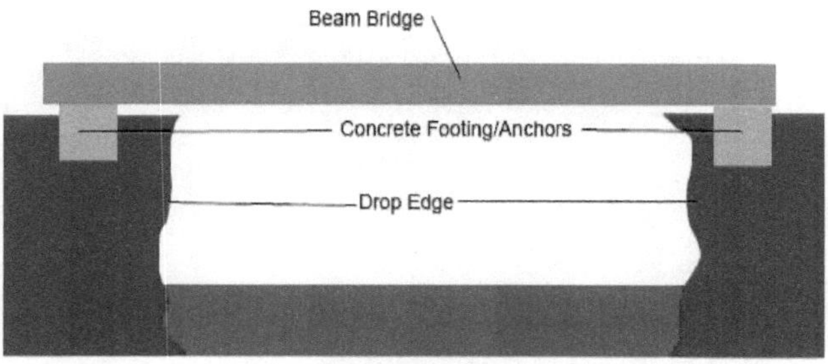

Fig.15.a

Beam Bridge Footing

The first step to making a bridge secure is to give it solid footing to start from, for our purposes we will be using concrete footings to attach our beam bridge to. After we have determined the width our bridge is going to be we can start by laying down the foundation framework to connect the rest of the bridge to. This is done by using concrete footings to attach the bridges supporting beams to. From the drop edge we are going to dig 2 holes on each side of the drop, sufficiently distanced from drop edge to ensure they will remain solid in the ground. These holes will serve as the foundation for our concrete footings. It is recommended to dig a hole at least 2 feet deep and 1-2 foot square for the base surface to which the support beams will rest on.

After the holes are dug, we will mix up our concrete mixture and pour into the holes. Ensure the surface area in which the beams will rest on is completely flat by using a trowel to smooth the surface area. Allow the concrete footings to dry completely before proceeding. Concrete takes quite a bit of time to cure completely, this can take a day or more.

After the footings have dried, we will now lay out our supporting beams. The beams must sufficiently reach the footings on both sides. We then measure the distance between the two beams on both sides to ensure the bridge beams run perfectly parallel to one another and do not increase or decrease in size from either side. After we have determined they are parallel to one another we then secure the beams to the concrete footings using steel straps.

We bolt the steel straps in place on the concrete footings to secure the beams in place. This is done on all 4 concrete footings to secure all ends of the 2 supporting beams. After we have secured the support beams in place to the footings we then lay out the bridge decking. (See Fig.15.b)

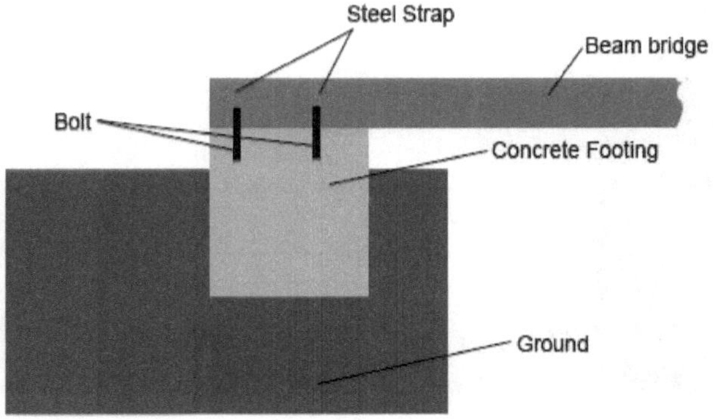

Fig.15.b

Using screws we will secure the bridge decking to the support beams. We recommend for bridge decking using wood a minimum of 2 inches in depth 2x4 / 2x6 planks work great for this. As you secure the decking to the beams ensure you allow a little bit of space between each board (1/8 inch) allowing for natural expansion of the wood in wet or hot conditions. It is extremely important to use fall protection while you secure the bridge decking as you will be required to gradually go further out on the bridge without anything below you to keep from falling. It is at this time, as you apply the bridge decking in place where you will wish to attach the guard rail posts in place as well; doing so in this step will make it much easier to connect as opposed to attaching them after the decking has been put in place. (See Fig.15.c & Fig.15.d)

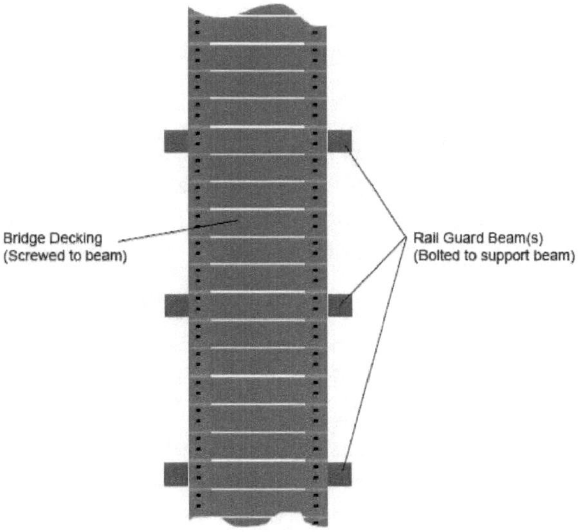

Fig.15.c

Top view of decking and rail guard beams

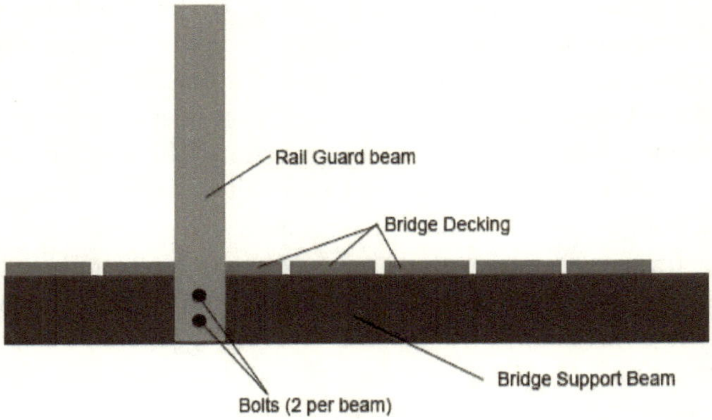

Fig.15.d

Side view of rail guard beams

Attaching the guard rail beams is relatively simple using a drill and bolts, drill the beams and bolt them to the bridges supporting beam. Using nuts and bolts securely fasten the rail guards to the supporting beams; you must use 2 bolts per rail guard to ensure stability.

Connecting beams can be tricky and can pose added safety concerns to a bridges design. Whenever possible it is always advised to use a single solid beam instead of numerous beams connected. However with longer spanning bridges this may not be possible and additional beams may be required to reach the entire span. If you must connect beams you need to ensure that the beams connection points are strong, as they will have a large load of weight to handle at any given time. Taking the 2 beams which need to be connected, also requiring 2 additional sections of beam (cut smaller) to fasten the beams together. The 2 beams will be laid out end to end and the smaller beam sections which will be used to secure everything together will be placed across the join area of the primary beams. They are then bolted into place using 2 bolts per beam end. 2 bolts are necessary to ensure the stability of the bridges design (4 bolts total per join). See Fig.15.e

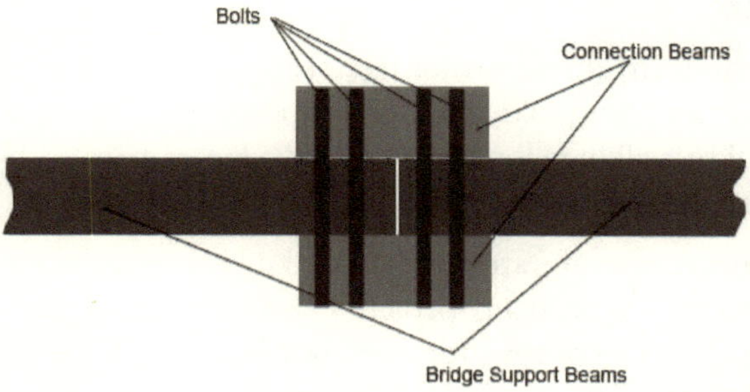

Fig.15.e

Rope Bridges

Of the many numerous bridge designs, no other seems to top the fun and enjoyment of an old fashioned rope bridge. There seems to be a sort of appeal to walking along a swaying bridge suspended by nothing but a couple ropes and simple planks of rope.

In this section we are going to detail how to build a rope bridge of your very own. As with any project which takes place above ground level there is always a concern for fall hazards, through the duration of construction of this bridge proper fall protection must be used at all times. Rope bridges by design are more unstable than static or fixed bridges; this has an added safety risk when using rope bridges. It is important to ensure the rope hand rails are tight and secure to provide the needed support to safely cross.

The basics to a rope bridge are that 2 ropes which have threaded wooden planks running through them are spanned across an opening or crossing and are fastened to each side. The supporting ropes must be strong enough to handle the weight load which will be placed on the bridge, including the weight of the wooden planks which will make up the walk way. Remember the heaver the persons crossing the thicker and stronger the rope must be. See Fig.16.a

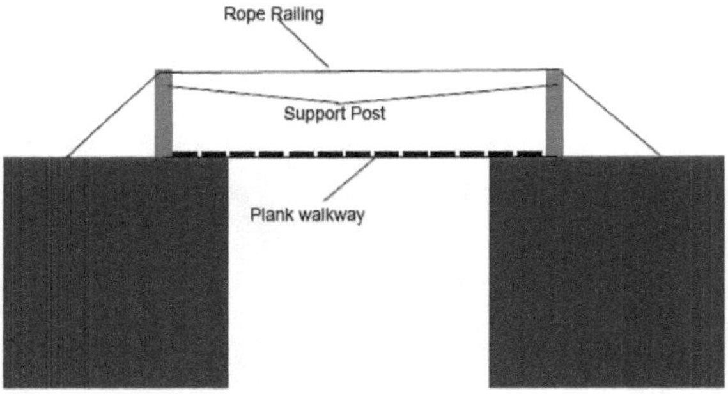

Fig.16.a

We first start by determining the location our Rope bridge is going to be located. If the bridges location is located on ground levels, we will use concrete footing as described in the previous section discussing Static beam bridges. If our rope bridge is going to be connected to arial platforms or other items, our method to connecting the supporting beams will be different (Usually by use of bolts to the frame) However the supporting beams no matter how they are anchored, must be strong and solid. See Fig.16.b

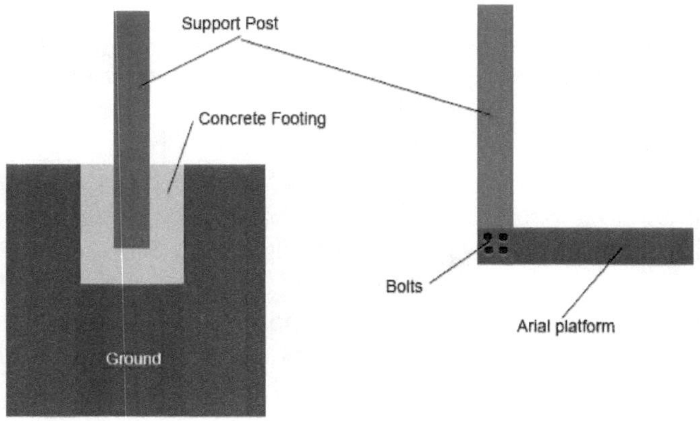

Fig.16.b

After we have setup out support post locations we will install and secure them in place, the distance recommended between the 2 support posts is 3-4 feet depending on the width of the planks width (we recommend a minimum of 3 feet width for the planks). After we have allowed the support posts to finish setting/ installation we can move on to the creation of the actual bridge portion. Using 2 lengths of rope of greater length than the intended span of the bridge, we will thread the wooden planks through to create the bridges platform. See Fig.16.c

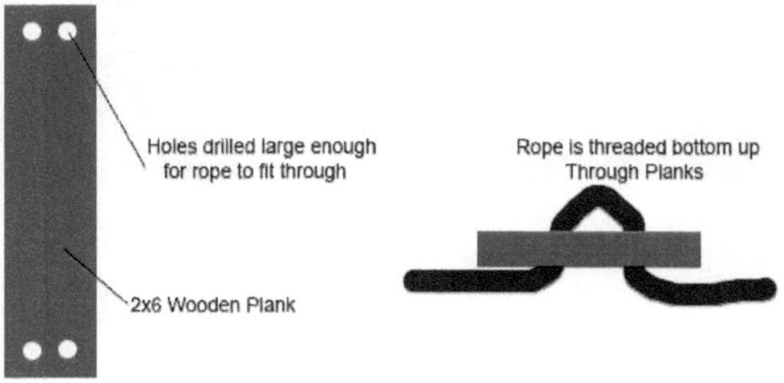

Fig.16.c

The rope is threaded through the planks to create the bridges platform. Rope is threaded from the underside up and then back down to the underside of the planks. This is done to ensure safety, in the case a planks center portion breaks or cracks, by threading underside up there is still some (however very little) support remaining. If a plank cracks or is broken it must be replaced immediately, as this poses a fall hazard.

After the bridges planks have all been threaded through we take the ends of the bridge and connect them to the supporting beams, securing one side entirely before the second. Ensure the Rope is pulled tight as it will slack with time and use, however do not over tighten; this can cause the rope to break. It is best to use fiber rope instead of nylon as nylon rope tends to stretch more and has a higher chance of breaking with time and use. After we have connected the rope platform to the supporting beams we now run the hand rails from the top of the support beams across as well, securing them to the platform and running along to the ground or platform level for added support. It is important to ensure the hand rail is tight with as little slack as possible as this will be the primary point for balance while crossing the bridge. We then run guide ropes from the handrail to the platform level to attach the rail to the bridge platform itself, this helps to add stability to the bridge and keeps the bridge and hand rail sagging at equal heights. The guide ropes are attached at distances of 2 feet apart equally across the entire span of the bridge. See Fig.16.d

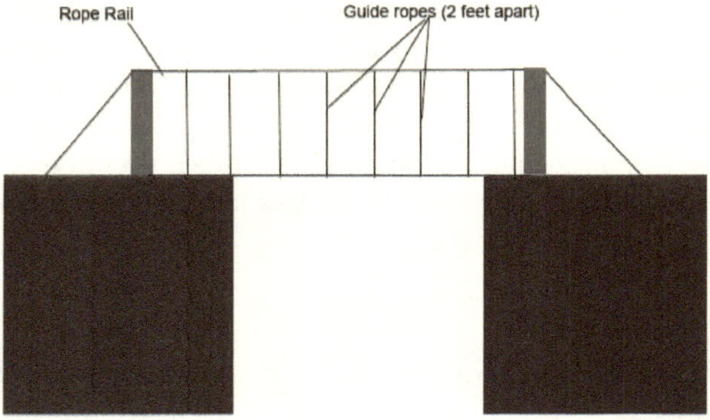

Fig.16.d

When building rope bridges, and initially testing them it is required to use fall protection. Always ensure the bridge ends are properly secured to the support posts, and posts are well anchored. With time it may be required to tighten the rope to keep the bridge from producing too much excess slack. The more slack on the rope platform the more the bridge will sway and swing with the wind. Routinely check and verify the bridge is in good working condition before allowing people to use the bridge. Replace or remove any portions of the bridge which become unsafe. Like all projects, there is never an excuse to skip steps or safety in building or using anything described in this book. Do not attempt to build bridges over extremely lengthy distances as the farther the bridge is, the less stability they offer to the end user.

Draw Bridges

Draw bridges are fun and bring out the knight in us all. The basis for this design of bridge is a Beam bridge which is statically connected to only one side. The draw side uses a hinge system to connect the bridge to the anchored spot. Using a cable system to connect the other side of the bridge allows for it to be raised and lowered with ease. The nice aspect to draw bridges is that they allow for control of passage. This can create a very reliable passage way which can be controlled who has access. IE – The draw side can determine who they lower the bridge for.

With all bridges there must be an anchored spot for the bridge to remain secured to. Although this can be one of many possibilities we will cover solid ground and arial platforms, as these are the 2 most common used. The bridges framework is near identical to a standard beam bridge with the exception of one side for the hinge connection point. See Fig.17.a

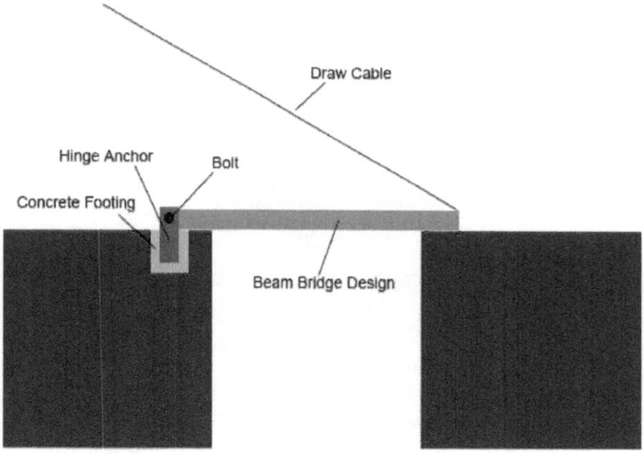

Fig.17.a

Note: For arial platform connections, the hinge is instead bolted to the platforms frame.

The hinge anchor is fairly simple in design; it consists of an anchored beam/post and a bolt to create a hinge between the anchored support beam and the bridge platform. The anchored beams are to be distanced the width of the beam bridge and ½ -1 inch extra spacing to allow for washers on the bolt assembly. The anchored beams should be on the outer sides of the bridge platform. The hinge connection should also be raised from ground level high enough so the bridge section does not hit. This ensures the bridge can be raised fully without complications. See Fig.17.b

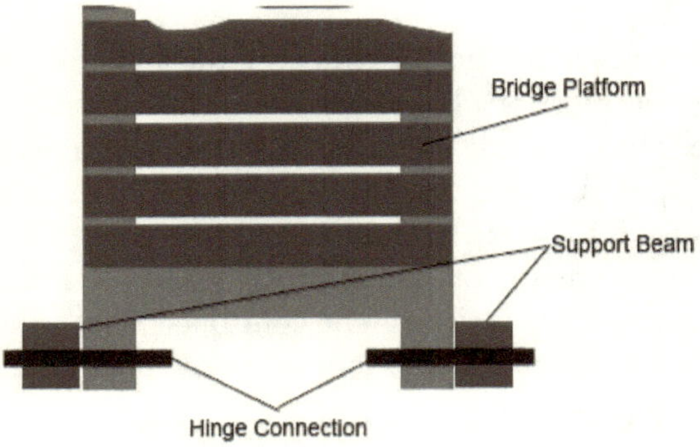

Fig.17.b

The draw cable system is consisted of a cable, and pulley system, to make raising and lowering the bridge section easy. The Initial pulley must be as high from the ground level as the bridge is in length. This ensures the platform can be pulled up with as minimal restraint from the bridge as possible. Depending on how the draw cable is to be utilized will determine how the system is connected. Ie – How it will be pulled and secured in place. For this we will assume a manual pull and secure. However with a little creativity you can create wheel, mechanized, or counterweight systems as well. See Fig.17.c

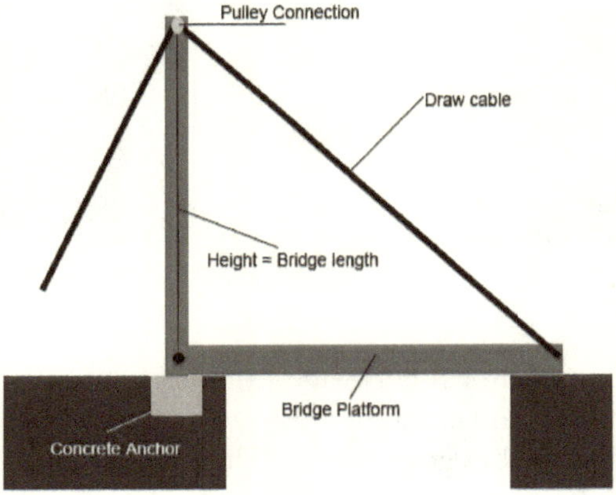

Fig.17.c

Draw bridges provide great fun for all ages, however it is important to routinely check the draw cable and bolt hinge systems to ensure they are in proper functional order before use. If any part of the bridge system faults, it must be replaced or removed immediately to ensure safety of the users.

Section 4

Secret Passages, Hidden Areas, Panic Rooms, And Secret Entrances.

Introduction to Secret/Hidden Areas

Every kid has grown up wishing they had a secret passage or room in their home. And for good reason, there is mystery and intrigue surrounding these secret and dark places. In this section we will discuss the basic principles and foundation to creating your very own hidden passageway or secret room.

The basics to any area that is hidden or secret is that basis, its kept secretive. Although most people do not have a real need to keep these areas secret. Perhaps just a way to hide cluttered closets or a kids play room. The first consideration to any area like this is the same. What is the area going to be used for, and how must security is required for that given area? If your uses are just to hide a cluttered extra storage room, then you obviously to not need state of the art locks and high security as a priority. If the area is to be used more in the fashion of a panic room or emergency shelter area then different considerations including structural and other security measures must be also brought in to consideration.

Regardless of its intended use, the same principles apply to concealing the entrance way. The entrance must blend in with the surrounding wall and room area to go unnoticed that there is an entry way to another section. This can be done in a number of methods and with a bit of creativity can be extremely effective. Some classic examples of a hidden entrance include book shelves, wall panels, faux (fake) flooring or any other number of possibilities. In this section we will detail and describe some of the more common methods to concealing an area or passage way.

Hidden Doorways/Entrances

The key to success for a hidden area or passageway is the entrance to the area. In general it is recommended that the door or entrance be off in an area which there is not heavy traffic. For example, not in a main hall way or room where many people would likely be. The more out of the way it is the better as there is less of a chance of the entrance way being accidently discovered. The door and frame are disguised in a manner which they will blend in with the surrounding room and wall. Book shelves, trophy mantles, wall cabinets are very effective methods to concealing an entrance way to a hidden area.

For the entrance way, the key element is to conceal the entrance "action" this is the door or handle latch, hinges and other items which would make it apparent there is more going on with the area than what is shown. The best goal to concealing the actions is to keep them on the side which is hidden. This being said most hidden entrances open inwards to the hidden areas as opposed to a normal door which may only open outwards. Another consideration which is vital to entrances success is ensuring it has the sufficient room to open and close properly. This is especially true with hinge entrances as unlike a typical door they will generally be larger and deeper in design (book shelf for example) The deeper the design, the more space is required to allow the entrance way to swing open freely without rubbing against the surrounding area.

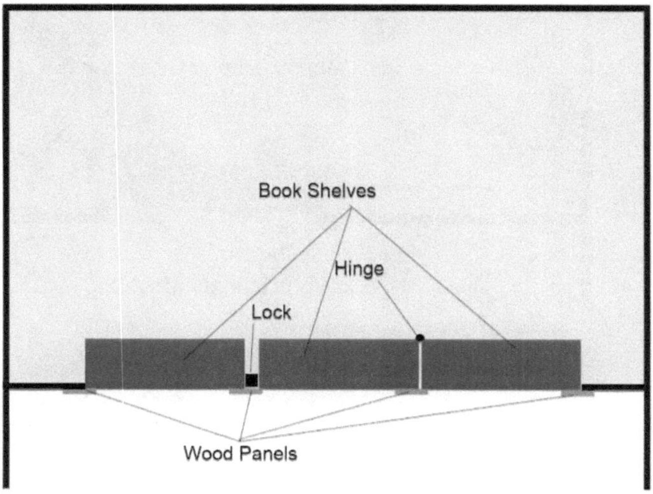

Fig.18.a – Book shelf hinge entrance (closed)

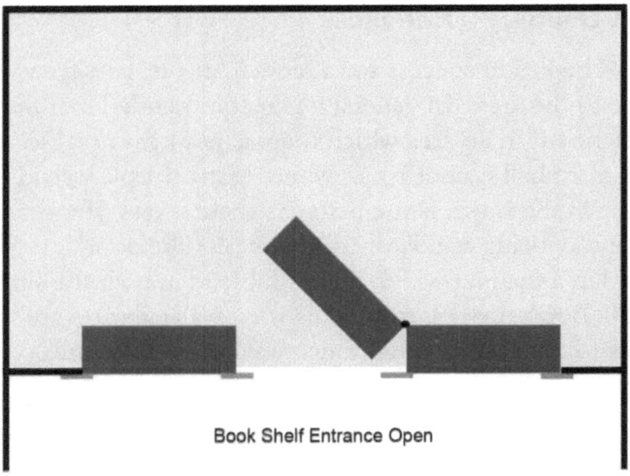

Fig.18.b – Book shelf hinge entrance (open)

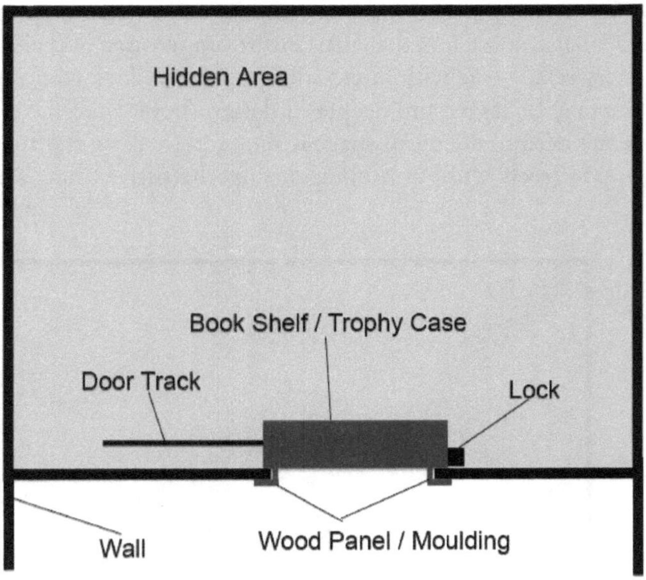

Fig.18.c – Book shelf sliding entrance (Closed)

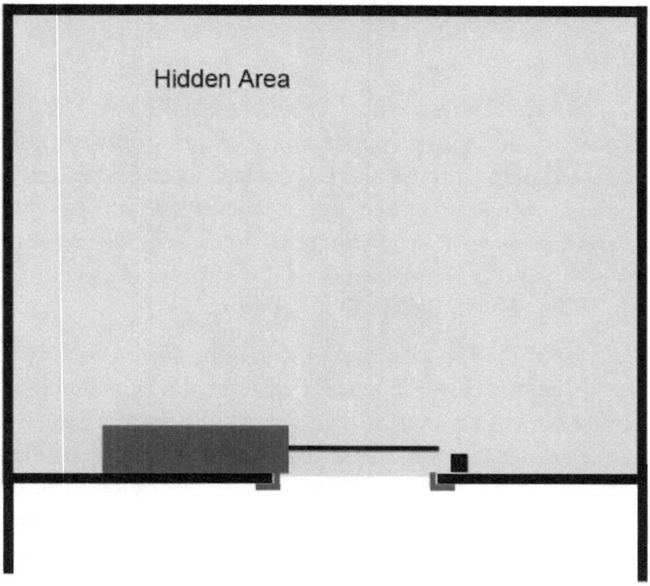

Fig.18.d – Book shelf sliding entrance (Open)

Hidden Door/Entrance Final Thoughts

Although the basic principles are the same for nearly any hidden entrances. The creativity put in by the designer will make the true success of a secret passageways entry truly impressive and above all successful in remaining secretive. So on that note, in the design stages be creative, you don't need to use a book shelf for the entry. Fake wall panels, trophy cases, mirrors and even furniture can be used to conceal an entry way to a hidden area. The previously noted examples are given to provide the basic framework to spark your own creativity and ingenuity. Although not covered in this book, Hydraulic or machine pumps and other systems can be implemented in to the design of the entry. More complex designs may require the use of such systems, so be prepared to consider them depending on your design.

Hidden Rooms/Areas

In this portion we will cover the basics to designing and creating the actual hidden area or room. A few considerations must be given in the design of these areas. Firstly is location, hidden areas are by design meant to remain concealed, this being said it is best to blend the room in to the design of the structure/house so it does not raise questions. Example – no corners of the room or area are visible on the exterior of the rest of the house or structure.

Size of the hidden area, although the size is not particularly important in many cases, in smaller structures it is generally recommended to keep the concealed area smaller, again so it does not raise suspicion as to why the remaining part of the structure is smaller than expected by the naked eye. Hidden/Secret passageways are not much different than the actual hidden area, although are generally kept smaller than a normal hall way, this is done to keep as much public area available and so the passage way does not take away from other rooms or amenities within the area. Passageways are in general roughly 2-3 feet in length wall to wall, or just enough space to move freely through the passage without feeling too cramped.

It is best to avoid windows and other tell tale signs of hidden areas. There is very little point in having a hidden room with a window in it, not only does it compromise the security of the hidden area, but from an external perspective, will become apparent there is a room or area where that window is located. Again why would you go through the trouble of installing a hidden passageway with a bookshelf entry when one could simply go through the window to access the area?

Sound! Nothing gives away a hidden area than someone hearing noise in a wall which is supposed to be solid or have nothing behind it. For this concern it is always recommended to use insulation within the walls of the hidden area to assist in noise reduction. This being said, it is further recommended against using noisy items such as sound systems, computers, or other agents which produce noise within the hidden area. Don't forget the ceiling and floors of the hidden area as well, just because you have insulated the walls does not mean the sound will not be heard from the upper or lower levels of the structure as well. Loud thumps on the hidden areas floors can and will echo down through the floor to the ceiling below.

Basic construction and home renovation knowledge is required to build these areas, unless the intended area is an existing room. Before proceeding further into this section we recommend doing a bit of research on interior framing, installing drywall and insulation. A poorly built hidden room will ruin the secretive nature of the area. It is also important to ensure the new addition blends well with the remaining portions of the structure, example – newly added wall or room matches in paint or wall paper of the remaining surrounding areas, same wall trim is used, etc…

In the following diagrams we will illustrate some examples of good placement and design of a hidden area. Again, these are simply examples and should be modified to best suit and tailor to your own personal desires and needs. In this example we are going to design a hidden area within a portion of the living rooms space with a entry to the area from the Study. Fig.19.a details a floor plan before the hidden area is built. Fig.19.b demonstrates the installation of the hidden area.

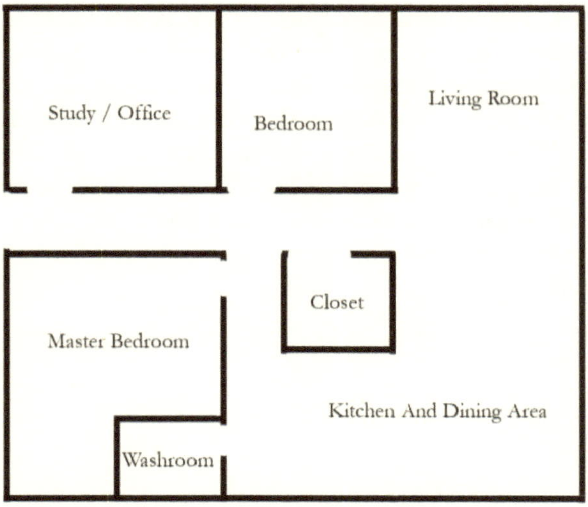

Fig.19.a – Floor plan before hidden area

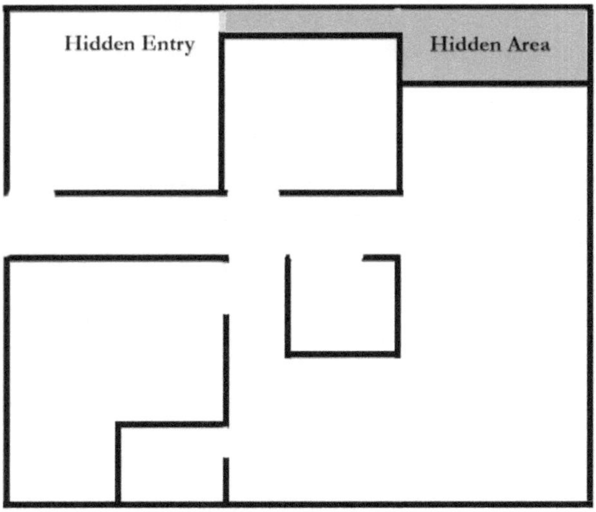

Fib.19.b – Floor plan after hidden area

As you will note in the above image, the hidden corridor is kept very narrow, as well as the hidden area. This is done to keep as much space in the main areas so it does not raise questions as to why rooms or areas are smaller than would be expected. It should also be noted that in this design the hidden area was kept away from critical areas that would involve a lot of back end plumbing and electrical, example – kept away from kitchen and bathroom areas. This is done primarily so critical items such as plumbing and electrical is not required to be reworked to fit the hidden area, also in the case a repair is required the hidden area is not exposed for the repairs.

Final Thoughts

Although a lot has been covered in this book, I still feel somewhere down the road I will end up writing another edition with more stuff to do, as I think of it. I would again caution people who attempt the items within this book. No matter how much you read and study, nothing can compensate for common sense and instinct. Many of these projects can be dangerous if not properly constructed or steps followed. Even with following safety protocols and building the best possible, there is always room for problems to surface. Be prepared for them as they arise. I would also like to take this opportunity to thank my friends and family for all the support which they have given me over the years. And my Son Paul, Daddy wrote this for you for when you get older. I hope we get to try all of these.

www.ingramcontent.com/pod-product-compliance
Lightning Source LLC
Chambersburg PA
CBHW020310290526
45784CB00003B/1450
9781257959013